DIVE DEEPER

DIVE DEEPER

THE HUMAN POETRY OF FAITH

MICHAEL PAUL GALLAGHER SJ

DARTON·LONGMAN+TODD

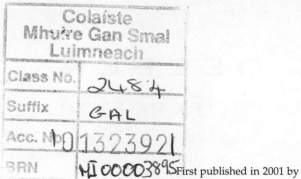
First published in 2001 by
Darton, Longman and Todd Ltd
1 Spencer Court
140–142 Wandsworth High Street
London SW18 4JJ

ISBN 0–232–52408–4

A catalogue record for this book is available
from the British Library.

Designed by Sandie Boccacci
Phototypeset in 9.5/13.25pt Palatino by Intype London Ltd
Printed and bound in Great Britain by
The Bath Press, Bath

CONTENTS

CHAPTER 1

IN TOUCH WITH
DEPTH

St Augustine says: *Make humanity your way and you shall arrive at God*. It is better to limp along that way than to stride along some other route.

(St Thomas Aquinas)

People become Christians because they discover Wisdom in Christianity . . . The poetry of good theology must grow from deep within the concrete experience of people.

(Rosemary Haughton)

To evoke our human adventure is the aim of this book. Its purpose is to make Christian faith more real through exploring our ordinary but deep experiences. Faith can be stifled by mere prose: it needs some touch of poetry to find its fire.

For many years I have sensed that the main blockage to Christian believing lies in our lifestyles and not in our ideas. The way we live can keep us adrift on the surfaces of ourselves and unable to reach deeper levels of searching. This happens within individuals. But it is also a cultural unfreedom, a shared cultural desolation. When we suffer from malnutrition in our self-images, we become incapable of imagining God. Look at the faces in the streets of any city. Many of them appear stressed, as if fighting to survive in a perpetual battle against time. Fragmentation and hyperactivity are the hallmarks, they say, of postmodernity. As Saul Bellow likes to ask, what does this do to our souls? What does it do to our spiritual imagination?

Our culture has difficulty with the antechambers of faith rather than with faith itself. It is on the level of disposition and desire that we need help most.

Other books I have written were more reliant on my reading. This time I want to give witness to a few truths that emerge from my listening to people over many years. For instance, there is often pain and confusion behind the mask of 'everything fine thanks'. But people also have a hidden poetry in them, not necessarily one that would find expression in writing, but a zone of imagination that is seldom recognised even by themselves. We live with unvisited spaces within ourselves, unknown not only to others but even to ourselves. It is hard to find the key on one's own. A certain quality of listening and presence is necessary to reach what Shakespeare called 'the melting mood'. When doors of imagination open to something of self-tenderness, we become ready for God.

So this book is about liberating our human depths so that we might be ready for the wonder of revelation, not forgetting that revelation also happens within seemingly 'non-religious' realities. God's Spirit is at work in all that is good. Like an artist, the Spirit shapes our entry into freedom on many levels. Therefore these pages explore the 'pre-religious' zone, where the Spirit works on us to lead us towards the fuller surprise of Christ.

'START FURTHER BACK'

Some years ago I gave a course for priests, dealing with the communication of faith today. After one of the sessions, a priest in his thirties came to talk to me. He told me about the difficulties he was experiencing in trying to reach the younger generation in his parish. He had set up opportunities of various kinds to reflect on faith. He had taken some of the main themes of the *Catechism of the Catholic Church* and tried to explain them in a way that might make sense to the young people. But he was disappointed. There was little response. People stopped coming. What should he have done? A little glibly I answered, 'Start further back'. 'What did you mean?' he asked. I explained my hunch that our crucial hungers are more human than explicitly religious: the language of the Catechism, even when well expounded, was not where the young people were 'at'. They needed a chance to discover their questions before being given any of the great answers of the Christian tradition. 'Start further back' meant not jumping into doctrinal language too early, or more positively, paying attention to the soil of experience into which the Sower has to sow today.

Even though I appreciated the young priest's desire to communicate the core truths of faith, his approach risked putting the cart before the horse. Religion too often jumps into the realm of creeds and codes. These dimensions are vital but they are not the starting point of the religious adventure. The Bible itself communicates on a non-doctrinal level – that of story, of experience, of slow discovery. This is the wavelength that this book wants to retrieve. It is more 'pre-religious' than 'religious'. It is more 'imaginative' than 'systematic'. It is more 'spiritual' than 'theological'. At its simplest it wants to evoke human experiences of depth and to ponder them as the theatre of the Spirit. It hopes to show that these encounter points with God are more frequent than we think – if we think only in narrowly 'religious' terms. There is a larger drama of growth through grace that is lived out in different ways in everyone.

Is this book shy of explicitly Christian faith? No and yes. No – because its hope is to move towards the reality of Christ through the drama of the Spirit in our lives. Yes – because it is afraid to start with familiar Christian words and images, which seem tired and unalive for so many people. This book would like to see itself as echoing the ministry of John the Baptist – in the sense of preparing the imagination of today for a fresh recognition of the Lord.

In the summer of 1999 I was asked to give a course for young adults in the Dolomite mountains of North Italy. I had been there two years previously when I had led twelve days on the theme of faith and unbelief, for about a hundred young Italians (largely between the ages of 20 and 30). Not all were 'believers' in a firm sense. Yet all were willing to give up part of their summer in order to reflect on their lives. Practically all my free time in the afternoons was taken with walking in the hills in conversation with individuals. I realised that the topics I was raising in the morning were relevant only when they were couched in terms of human experience. I learned that I had to leave aside the typical language of theology and to connect the struggles of faith to ordinary life and especially to the realm of relationships. It became clear that when I used stories or slides or symbols or some mention of my own inner struggles, what I was seeking to communicate came alive.

For my return visit I needed a new theme. I proposed the title 'Growing through Imagination', with the idea of drawing on the arts as a source of preparing the way for faith. I chose some major existential issues – like friendship or failure or suffering or solitude – and I tried to find examples from literature or drama or cinema to embody them imaginatively. It proved a fruitful entry to spirituality for those young people. And so I decided to write this book – not to repeat the same material – but to explore similar avenues towards depth. Five chapters call on some of the literary geniuses of the past in order to evoke the multi-layered drama that we live. Later sections cross the threshold into the surprise that is Christian revelation, ending with a chapter of more ambitious theological horizons. The problem is that many people have encountered the Christian vision only in tired language and in frozen forms. The hope here is to awaken the sleeping beauty of our wonder so that we can be more ready for the greater wonder that is Jesus Christ.

INTENDED READERS

There must be all these people everywhere on Earth, so *desperate* for just the smallest sign that there is something finer or larger or more miraculous about ourselves than we had supposed. How can I give them a spark?

(Douglas Coupland, *Girlfriend in a Coma*, 1998)

My last book, *Clashing Symbols*, was the most 'academic' that I had written, with plenty of footnotes and fairly dense explanations of theories of culture. Some friends of mine were disappointed. They had expected me to write in the same vein as previous books like *Free to Believe*, which sought to trace spiritual journeys in a personal tone. Many of them told me that the epilogue of *Clashing Symbols* was the best part of it. It was an afterthought where I recounted a visit to my native village in Co. Sligo accompanied by some Italian friends, which spurred me to reflect on the drama of changing cultures. I was told that I should have written the whole book in that way, mixing lived situations with religious reflection.

Dive Deeper tries to obey the desire of those readers. Instead of being 'academic', it is intended to give priority to the imaginative or poetic in all of us. For about twenty years I lectured on modern literature in Ireland's largest state university. In 1990 I moved to Rome where I began to teach theology. My initial plan for this book was to study the links between literature and theology, as if building a bridge between two sides of my own life. But many authors have examined the religious dimensions of literature in terms of its 'philosophy'. I wanted to approach the dialogue between faith and imagination differently. Great literature creates, and demands, a certain receptive wavelength in us. Real reading means allowing ourselves to be changed by the experience itself, not just by its content. Literary criticism and theology are second-order activities, analysing experience. But the encounter with literature, like the encounter with faith,

requires some contemplative conversion in us. If that disposition of wonder remains undernourished, we cannot enter the
kingdom either of imagination or of spirituality.

Imagination is the zone where religious faith and artistic
creativity meet. Artists have always been hesitant about ab-
stractions. Their calling is to the concrete drama of life and they
specialise in speaking to our intuitive levels of consciousness:
they hit us below the belt of reason. They awaken wonder and
develop it into wisdom. They confront pain by going further
into depth. The whole area that art evokes is the area that religion most needs and often fails to reach. In that spirit I draw on
some major imaginative writers, taking some classic moments in
literature as dramatising crucial thresholds that we face.

There is a haunting line at the end of T. S. Eliot's *The Waste
Land*: 'these fragments I have shored against my ruins'. We are
all aware of the ruins around us: the end of an era, the collapse
of many traditions, the uncertainty about our roots, the loss of
religious anchors, the scepticism about any possible wisdom,
and the larger shadow of a world often in terrible pain. But my
life has taught me to believe both in humanity and in God. The
exploratory nature of these pages is meant to capture the
unsteady roads of our seeking. They are stabs at a vision, point-
ers at a surprise, avenues towards hope and love and faith – perhaps in that order. Faith itself is a God-given way of imagining
existence – not a cold truth, easily captured in concepts. And my
conviction is that imaginative writers, like biblical prophets, can
deepen our angle of seeing.

It is strange to be writing a book of this kind in Rome during
the year of the Great Jubilee. The city is full of pilgrims who may
not need a book of this sort. Most of them are probably at home
in the faith expressions of the Church. Many have found a language of committed Christianity through some movement or
parish community. They are the privileged ones of today's spiritual scene – those who retain roots in a traditional religion and
who have managed to renew their sense of God through official
channels. Their starting point for faith lies in believing and

belonging, in being nourished through the sacraments and in embodying their vision in good works of many kinds. These pages might be of interest to the Jubilee pilgrims but they are not my main audience. I write this book for those more on the margins. Like St Paul opting to give priority to a ministry for the Gentiles, we need a spirituality of searching for those who are frequently put off by Church language and who feel themselves disappointed and undernourished by their surrounding culture.

Inevitably there are several important dimensions of faith that will not receive much attention in these pages. One in particular deserves mention. Nearly a hundred years ago the American thinker Josiah Royce wrote: 'My life means nothing, either theoretically or practically, unless I am a member of a community.' This serves as a wise reminder that although the tone of these pages is personalist, our human roads towards light are never just private. The normal and blessed context for finding Christian faith is within a church belonging. I am writing for those on the inside of church in the hope of enriching their human basis for faith, but my hope is to reach those outside church belonging who walk more lonely paths of honest searching.

SPIRITUAL CATECHUMENS

Many young people today feel themselves deprived of community supports. They may admit to a sense of self-emptiness and life-without-goals, but they often despise what seem to them the over-easy answers of religion. I have stopped counting the number of times when young adults have expressed what I would call their 'cultural desolation'. From people with very different backgrounds I have heard variations on this theme. What they say goes something like this:

'In this society it's impossible to be oneself. Superficiality reigns. Appearance is everything. I'm sure there are people out there who are as unhappy with these trivial games as I am but how can I find them? Anything serious is laughed at. Interest in religion is viewed as "weird". If I express anything that goes beyond the usual agenda of pleasure, pastimes, success, career, money, sex, holidays and so on, I'm looked on as strange, even as threatening. The result is that I lose trust in my own hopes. It's easier to throw in the sponge and settle for "the way things are". But that is self-betrayal. So I'm caught between two worlds. Some of my hopes have been dented. I wonder how I'll find a marriage partner who is not infected with this falsity. I live with dull disappointment all the time. It's a lonely road. But there must be more than this.'

In this light, my ideal reader for these chapters is what I would call a spiritual or cultural catechumen of today. In the early centuries of Church history there were programmes for those moving towards baptism. Today many of the baptised, through no fault of their own, are catechumens in a different sense. They have never arrived at a decision of faith. Often they have never been invited in a way that made sense to them. They swim in today's culture, burdened by sheer complexity and wounded by a lopsided way of imagining our humanity. Some of them suffer from the desolations voiced just now. For them I chose to write this book, based on the conviction that we often need to get in touch with ourselves before we can be ready to hear the surprise of God.

To such a person I would say: 'If God or religion seems in a fog for you, try another route towards the threshold of faith. You need time to listen to your own human depths, with imagination and quiet. Yes, the superficial culture can block what your heart desires. A choice is required to resist the pressures and find space. If you create a more personal space, what major concerns will surface for you? Relationships and the path of love. Some sense of self-disappointment and guilt. A feeling of impotence because of the tragedies of our divided planet. A longing for stillness where some spiritual awareness could be nourished. A search for anchors within the scattered life of everyday.'

Our next five chapters will explore those five areas of concern. At the end of those chapters, and of some others, the theme will be expanded through a mini-anthology of quotations.

IMAGINATION AS KEY

The real battles of life take place within the human imagination (as Cardinal Newman argued over a century ago). How do we see ourselves? What do we hope for? What is it all about? The deeper answers, whether positive or negative, are found in how we imagine our lives, not just in how we think about them. It is on that level that we find either anchors of wisdom or else suffer from dispersion and emptiness. Faith is a form of imagination (which is not to say that it is imaginary). Faith takes many forms, not just the official religious ones. It is a language of trust and of meaning. It seeks to express itself in some belonging and commitment. But most of all, it shapes and is shaped by our imagination.

This book is born from worry over the deadness that marks much 'religious' language. Many of our sermons are couched in predictable words, sadly lacking in imagination. Much well-intentioned religious discourse remains lazy and listless. 'Where there is no vision, the people perish', said Proverbs (29:18). The failure of conventional religion is that it does not evoke the spiritual roots of our journeying. It assumes that everyone can hear the scriptures 'neat', or enter the wavelength of the liturgy without difficulty. Instead many people are nowhere near the threshold of such readiness. They are untouched by ceremonies that were forged for another culture. They are in need of a more sensitive initiation to their own spiritual drama. As St Paul might say, they need milk before meat.

My more positive starting point is the desire to do justice to our human hungers. We have a natural desire for God. Which means that our hearts are always on the watch-out for vision, love, fullness, surprise – if only we can emerge from the prisons of our smaller concerns. There is a readiness for the real God within us, not fulfilled by the god of complacent religion.

'There must be more than this.' This book wants to show that there is more than this *within our grasp*. Within ordinary human experience are untapped sources of wonder. Within easy reach of anyone is a different way of seeing things. I have been amazed to find how relatively effortless it is to open doors of new imagination for people. It is as if many of us are simply waiting for someone to come along with a key or a mirror – in order to open a door, or to see one's depth. Jesus delighted in offering people freedom from their many prisons.

A true episode can provide a closing parable for this introduction. Last summer I was teaching a course in Fordham University, New York, and living in the Jesuit community house on campus. One day I wanted to go from the basement to the third floor and decided to take the elevator. I pressed the button marked '3'. The doors closed but nothing happened. Tried again. No movement. Pressed the button to open the doors. Nothing. With mounting anxiety I tried buttons '1' and '2'. No result at all. I was about to sound the alarm bell but gave it one last try and pressed '4'. Off it went. I got out, feeling very relieved, and walked down the stairs to level three, using my house key to enter the corridor. Later I mentioned my escapade to some of the community. 'But don't you have the key?' was the answer. Sure enough, with the keys I had been given there was a small one that I had not noticed. It was for the elevator, for those floors not open to the public. I had the key but I did not know it.

The parable does not need much commentary. We can live in a more limited space than God intends for us. Perhaps our lives get programmed to visit only a few floors in the skyscraper that is our humanity. If so, we move within a fraction of our real selves. And ironically we have the key all the time, without realising it. This book draws attention to neglected floors in our human adventure, and suggests that by visiting our ordinary humanity with wonder, we may find ourselves drawn towards the larger Mystery of our existence.

Imagination is the key to hope. The poetry of God is calling for new expressions. Because God does not speak in boring prose, moralistic messages, routine rituals, but in soaring imaginative love, in events of liberating surprise from exodus to resurrection. To renew the freshness we need to dive deeper.

open a door: see one's depth

Key

CHAPTER 2

THE GATEWAY OF FRIENDSHIP

Such a friend. It almost made me shy to think of it.

(Seamus Deane)

What zone of our lives shapes our imagination most? Perhaps the varied spectrum of friendship is the place where we discover ourselves through the changing phases of life. It can be a space of quiet mutual confidence and of dramatic breakthrough. It is capable of causing deep hurts and of reaching beyond them into honesty and forgiveness. Friends spur hearts beyond smallness and towards the promised land of who we can become. Friendship can mean exodus and fidelity together, and then it is the human basis of the other exodus and fidelity called religious faith.

The epigraph comes from an account by Seamus Deane, writer and critic (and my colleague for many years), of his long companionship with Nobel laureate Seamus Heaney. In an article in *The New Yorker* in March 2000 he recalls a road accident in Dublin in 1976 when his car ran into a lamp-post while avoiding a swerving motorcyclist. Heaney was driving just behind and 'a very upset poet' helped Deane out of his car: 'It had been a close call.' Later over strong tea Heaney seemed to go into shock and began talking in the dialect of his childhood: 'Och, aye'. 'Man, dear'. Deane concluded: 'When I saw his shock and distress again, [he was] such a friend. It almost made me shy to think of it.' This vignette beautifully captures one aspect of friendship – its often unvoiced tenderness and yet its capacity to last over many years.

At the reception to celebrate my ordination, I ended my speech by quoting a few lines of W. B. Yeats. They came from the end of his poem 'The Municipal Gallery Revisited', where he looks around at the portraits in the gallery and realises that so many of these people had been his personal friends:

> Think where man's glory most begins and ends,
> And say my glory was I had such friends.

Friendship was described by Thomas Aquinas, an un-Romantic genius if ever there were one, as 'the source of greatest joy'. Without friends, he added, even the most fulfilling activities become empty. Friendships are spaces where our capacity for life is nourished by others. We discover how to trust and how to be trusted. We learn to open up in wonder and to find new worlds in us that are brought to birth by the presence of another.

Over these thirty years I've had to learn that there are very different languages of mutual presence. There is a joy and a cost in our being present to one another. But our quality of life is measured by our skill in mastering those languages, by the ease and fluency of our being present – to ourselves, to others, and, ultimately, to God.

The greatest satisfaction of my life as a priest has come from the space I have tried to create for people in search of healing or hope. I used to feel a little guilty over other kinds of priestly service that I may have been neglecting. But we only have one life to live. I was not called to frontline social ministry, even though I twice volunteered to go to other continents. For most of the time I was in university contexts that did not give priority to the sacramental celebration of faith. But I have always relished contact with people in search of some light on their life. Again and again I discovered 'presence' as a befriending space, a healing place, like an unofficial sacrament of our humanity.

FROM INTENSITY TO PRESENCE

When I made that speech as a newly ordained priest, I was young. I thought of friendship in terms of mutual closeness and sharing, and of a certain excitement in being together. Now I feel things differently. That dimension of emotional intensity remains vital but it is no longer at the centre. Perhaps the greatest gift we can offer one another is not intimacy but something subtler, less pressing: a certain quality of presence and fidelity through changes.

We are 'relational' beings, philosophers tell us. How we relate to one another is central to who we are. If this language in us goes tired, we slide into 'living and partly living' (T. S. Eliot). If we discover new wavelengths of presence, then our hearts and imaginations will find their essential nourishment. Is there any genuine and lasting human growth unconnected with relationships?

In this context, over years, what I might call my pastoral credo has emerged: people are hungry for a different space of self-hearing and self-healing, and when they find it they spontaneously start looking for God. In the experience of human presence and relationship we glimpse the gateway into a mystery that surrounds us – that we live and move within another Presence and are invited into another Relationship.

An example may illustrate this credo. Alan was a brilliant engineering student who entered a serious depression which left him unable to study. His parents proved unhelpful. His father told him that he was 'useless' and a disgrace to the family. His mother retreated into embarrassed denial, pretending that everything was as before. He was sent to a psychiatrist who probed around and prescribed tablets. Alan felt treated as an object. He tried to force himself to study. His friends did not know how to respond and kept their distance. Alan's confusion and frustration increased. He became obsessive about cleanliness and counting money. When he talked to me, compulsively, I realised that I was out of my depth. I listened to extended diatribes against himself and all those around him. Then one day, when the rage and the fury had been exhausted, a different tone began to emerge. I was able to say, you are in touch with another side of yourself now, a more gentle and fragile self, less resentful and more trusting.

Alan had reached that 'different space' of my 'credo'. Again and again I have seen people arrive at this threshold. Beyond the turmoil, a tenderness. Beyond the anger and bitterness, something akin to forgiveness. This space is born from honesty – and from the presence of another person who is not afraid of a slow journey through the desert. Indeed, when Alan had reached and recognised this gentler tone, he began to talk about faith, about being afraid of God and yet wanting to pray. We went together to the chapel, where we sat at ease in front of an icon, and another Presence became real to us beyond all our words.

Of course Alan's story is more complex. A book could be written about it. I am trying only to indicate a simple human truth about what we can offer to one another – in friendship, in presence, in space, in relationships of different kinds. This dimension of our lives is a crucial springboard for all kinds of 'faith'.

AN EXAMPLE FROM FICTION

[Austen's novels] encourage us to know ourselves and to judge others rightly.

(Eva Brann)

Emma is Jane Austen's most ambitious novel, involving a series of conversions of heart in its heroine. The opening paragraph is famous for an ironic sharpening of knives on the part of the narrator. She likes her central character but Emma has a lot to learn before she can cross the threshold into loving and being loved:

> Emma Woodhouse, handsome, clever, and rich, with a comfortable home and happy disposition, seemed to unite some of the best blessings of existence; and had lived nearly twenty-one years in the world with very little to distress or vex her.

As in every Austen novel, the plot moves through obstacles towards married love; in this case those obstacles are within Emma's character, which is outwardly so lively but in reality dangerously flawed. On the same first page we are told of 'unperceived' 'evils' in her 'disposition' including 'the power of having rather too much her own way'. The text gleefully undermines this egoism, in a series of satiric humiliations, until Emma is at last able to love and be loved. Her early blunders have to do with others. Emma's 'love of match-making' leads her into a situation where she wants Mr Elton, the snobbish clergyman, to become involved with Harriet Smith, her protégé. Instead he falls for Emma and makes 'violent love to her'!

This is the first 'deep mortification' of Emma's ego. Austen delights in revealing the cleverness and self-complacency that renders deep mutual relationships impossible. Other exposures follow but only in the third volume of the book is Emma painfully set free for love. To adopt the vocabulary of spiritual wisdom, her liberation goes through purgative, illuminative and unitive stages. The purgative crisis takes place on a picnic outing that proves 'downright dullness' for Emma. Austen brilliantly describes the mounting frustration of the whole group as they experience 'a languor, a want of spirits'. Eventually Frank Churchill (the leading socialite) proposes a game: each person is to amuse Emma by saying 'one thing very clever', or 'two things moderately clever, or three things very dull indeed'. The kindly chatterbox Miss Bates, a middle-aged lady who had known better times, remarks in all innocence, 'I shall be sure to say three dull things as soon as ever I open my mouth'. In Austen's world basic dispositions are often revealed in the smallest of incidents and this is a classic one:

> Emma could not resist.
> 'Ah! Ma'am, but there may be a difficulty. Pardon me – but you will be limited as to number – only three at once'.

The barb strikes home and Miss Bates is deeply hurt. More important, Emma's claws have been noticed by all and in particular by Mr Knightley, her close friend and mentor. Her irritation and boredom had tempted her to let her cruel side be seen. The picnic staggers to its close. When Emma is about to depart, Knightley confronts her:

> 'How could you be so unfeeling to Miss Bates? How could you be so insolent in your wit to a woman of her character, age, and situation? Emma, I had not thought it possible.'

And on the basis of being her friend, he voices his shock over her 'pride of the moment'. In silence Emma experiences 'anger against herself, mortification and deep concern'. 'She felt it at her heart.' She goes home, 'tears running down her cheeks . . . extraordinary as they were'. Using overtly religious language Austen describes Emma's 'true contrition' as she decides to visit Miss Bates the next day.

This is act one of her conversion. A more illuminative stage comes when she realises that Harriet, whom she had been grooming for Frank Churchill, in fact has her eyes on Mr Knightley!

> A few minutes were sufficient for making her acquainted with her own heart . . . She touched – she admitted – she acknowledged the whole truth . . . It darted through her with the speed of an arrow, that Mr Knightley must marry no one but herself!

This insight leads to another day of 'humiliation' over her 'unpardonable arrogance'. Apart from 'her affection for Mr

Knightley, every other part of her mind was disgusting'. When next they meet, the tone between them is new. They gradually admit their love. The change is complete. Unitive wonder is now possible between them. 'This one half hour had given to each the same precious certainty of being beloved' – even though as Austen comments, 'very seldom does complete truth belong to any human disclosure'.

From the Emma of the opening, who was so cock-sure and protected from pain, the novel thus arrives at an Emma in need of forgiveness and open to tenderness. There is no big drama. Everything important takes places within the small circle. Austen seems to insist that we grow most within the ordinary and through learning – with true friends – to see through our many self-deceptions. Her story is almost a parable of how real friendship prepares the path towards love. In friendship the shadows are faced, self-deceptions are overcome, and quite simply people are liberated from themselves. A friend is one who can see the shadows and then be a mirror for us of so much more than our shadows.

DIALOGUE ON
RELATIONSHIPS

Go deeper than love, for the soul has greater depths,
love is like the grass, but the heart is deep wild rock
molten, yet dense and permanent.

(D. H. Lawrence)

To put Jane Austen and D. H. Lawrence in dialogue on this theme of relationships must seem an eccentric choice. Even allowing for the fictitious nature of the encounter, they have totally opposed temperaments and worldviews. It is a confrontation between the refined and the feverish imagination. Lawrence once dismissed Austen as a 'mean old maid' incapable of showing passion. He could well have said of her what he wrote in *Women in Love*: 'She never really lived, she only watched.'

In recent years Austen, however, has undergone a revaluation by the critics as well as a surge in popularity through the cinema. She is seen as quietly 'subversive' (the word is from W. H. Auden). She has been acclaimed by the philosopher Alasdair MacIntyre as the 'last great effective imaginative voice' of traditional ethics: she sniffed out the danger of a modern self devoted to appearance rather than rooted in virtue. Feminist commentators interpret her as embodying a 'regulated hatred' of male culture and its falsity. Indeed for many people today Austen is more stimulating than Lawrence. He sounds plodding and ideological in his insistence that 'the flesh is wiser than the intellect'. Even his famous dramatisations of the undercurrents of human sexuality can seem dated. Nevertheless he is unique among novelists in his ambition to face conflictual feelings between people, in what he called their 'pre-cognitive flow' prior to all words. If Austen relished the complexity of conscious life, Lawrence shifted his focus towards less conscious and more fearful areas of struggle within relationships.

Lawrence was agonizingly aware that a new externalist culture was cramping our emotions. In his own words, 'the old consciousness has become a tight-fitting prison for us, in which we are going rotten'. 'Man is the only creature who has deliberately tried to tame himself. He has succeeded.' 'We have lost touch with our deeper needs in a kind of madness.' 'What we want most is living wholeness, not isolated salvation.' Thus he put his finger on a crisis concerning intimacy: is the self-energy everything or is there some greater mystery within which our fulfilment finds roots and harmony?

In spite of all their obvious divergences, both writers delve into the hidden movements that underlie relationships. By diverse routes they move through various layers of resistance towards the freedom to love another person. Although their basic philosophies could hardly be more at variance, these two novelists have some common ground. In this conversation their convergences and their tensions can highlight aspects of the interpersonal adventure that is so crucial in shaping who we become. As in dialogues in later chapters, no claim to accuracy is intended. Indeed one might usefully think of 'Austen' and 'Lawrence' as names in inverted commas, and this is especially true of later parts of their conversation where they go beyond what we know of the horizons and views of these two authors. Phrases in italics are more or less direct quotations.

Risks and barriers

JA: We seem utterly different but we both wrote about the complexity of human relationships.

DHL: In opposite ways. I hated your stories because they scratched the social exterior of life and never explored the murky and magnificent underworld of passion between men and women.

JA: Do you still think of me as a silly female doodling with surface matters?

DHL: I see more subtlety than before, but I still think that you magnified minor flaws into major crises and that you never faced people's more volcanic emotions.

JA: You preferred the big brush strokes. I opted for the small-scale portrait, working on *'two inches wide of Ivory'*. We were both fascinated by what goes on in people as they move into relationships, in areas that they themselves don't recognise. Someone described my novels as an extended pre-marriage course! You too wanted to show people on a journey towards the freedom to love.

DHL: Relationships do not just happen – we have to learn how to open towards tenderness.

JA: We have to unlearn a lot of pride and prejudice before we arrive at the beginning of love.

DHL: We long for closeness but we run from the risks involved. The very approach of intimacy is a source of fear.

JA: The first risk is within ourselves. We cling to our little ego and see others as existing to fit our plans.

DHL: I preferred to expose the power-driven ego.

JA: In my own way, I was there before you. When people are blocked within themselves, or twisted by snobbery, they are unready for surrender. My Emma, for instance, had to have her ego-lenses shattered before she could be in touch with her heart.

DHL: But you put the conscious ego too much at the centre of the stage. There is no room for our strangeness. You ignore the darker forces that emerge when we enter zones of intimacy.

I wanted to show the power games typical between men and women. They stumble into minefields of mutual war because each wants to dominate.

JA: My focus was on the barriers to love, not on the continuing drama of loving. I saw real love as endangered in the new culture around. There was an older culture where the self learned values from beyond one's individual horizon. Then came the new urban mentality. In my books any character who likes London symbolises a drifting disposition. He or she represents a self without anchors. If it feels right, it must be right. If the social appearances are acceptable, what could be wrong? My passion was to satirise this lifestyle as rootless and as trivialising the road towards love.

Beyond the interpersonal

DHL: I too was reacting to a crisis in my time. I saw the world around me as sick. People seemed monopolised by their possessive will-power, or caught in silly games of sexual pleasure. *When we make an ideal of love, or an understood thing, we make a mess of it.* As a result they were cut off from their real fountains of life, from the spontaneous 'religious' impulses within us.

JA: In what sense religious? I thought you saw church religion as a dead force.

DHL: It is a dead force only if it fails to do justice to mystery or energy. I was more religious than you, more passionate about the revelation of God in the drama of who we are. You recognised a crisis in culture, but you saw this as ethics, not as religion. Your characters were too self-enclosed in their consciousness. You ignored the larger mystery: when we arrive at genuine passion we reach a kind of 'God-knowledge', in the shimmering flow of mutual wonder.

JA: You gave too much attention to the 'dark gods'. In my view people are more often victims of socially induced egoism.

DHL: But egoism has deeper roots. It is never just personal pettiness. It is part of a tragedy of forgetfulness. Our capacity for love is more than an opening out of one individual to another. I am appalled by the narrowing of man-woman relationships to the merely sexual or to a cul-de-sac of separate selves seeking fulfilment. According to you I gave too much attention to the underworld. I think you paid too little attention to the terrors and transformations of human loving.

JA: I preferred to watch people escape from their psychological unfreedom. That too is a transformation needed for mature love.

DHL: But there is more than the social or the psychological. *We are related to the universe in some religious way, prior to any relationship with one another.* Our lives and loves belong to something larger than ourselves. We are perishing in our separation from *the great sources of our inward nourishment, sources that flow eternally in the universe. In this vast whole I am a small part.*

JA: Your language is certainly not mine. But I fear a culture where individuals are left to their lonely selves and told that inter-personal love is the goal of their lives. The space they are given is too small and, yes, what is missing can be called 're-ligious'. I saw genuine love as conversion and openness, never as mere self-discovery.

DHL: Conversion to what?

JA: To a sense of wonder that my life is called beyond the horizon of my little self. What starts with companionship and blossoms into friendship, into what you call deeper desires.

Sources of healing

DHL: The long adventure of tenderness is where most people emerge from their fears. I look on it as a lifelong space of healing.

JA: Healing from what, would you say?

DHL: From the accumulated bruises of existence. Which of us is born into a perfect family situation? Early on we learn to mask our hostilities and to protect our vulnerability. Mature love is the place where that damage can be repaired. More than that, *marriage keeps me in communication with the unknown, where otherwise I would be lost.*

JA: So you think that love between a man and a woman is the greatest source of human flourishing?

DHL: Yes, when it has the courage to cross thresholds and not flinch from crises. There is a violence that is always possible between people. We are a *mixture of yea and nay, a rainbow of love and hate.*

JA: There are also spaces of quiet recognition, where those dangers disappear. Their place is taken by reverent amazement that you are completely at home with this other person. There comes to birth a giving and receiving that is akin to prayer.

DHL: That breakthrough into blessedness is what I was calling healing spaces. But they remain fragile. Many shadows can threaten all that beauty. Within relationships we are capable of terrible destructiveness. You always have both *the kissing and the striving.*

JA: Surely *the* threshold is to face the full range of who we are and to face it with the loved friend. It means embracing the saint and the demon in the other person. 'For better, for worse' as the marriage ceremony says.

DHL: Yes, that is the hurdle where many fall. Crossing that threshold goes beyond merely comfortable images of love.

JA: A capacity for forgiveness deepens faithfulness. I am always amazed if somebody comes to accept me, to the point of forgiving my darker days and my selfish sides.

DHL: Only then do we arrive at the deepest fidelity that deserves to be called love. Intimacy can be an exciting discovery. But a tenderness that embraces the shadows needs a slow blossoming over years. That is the real measure of our adventure with one another.

Recognition as surprise

JA: The magic moment is one of recognition. It comes when two people realise that something precious is awakening between them.

DHL: They step outside the bounds of their previous selves and of their conditioning. They dare to cross frontiers of feeling and of poetic fire. All of existence is seen differently, because they are emotionally alive.

JA: They awaken not just feelings but a sense of goodness in each other. Life is seen with grateful eyes.

DHL: But there is also a volcanic side to love, something awesome in its power. You come alive in ways never imagined.

JA: Before the volcanic passion comes the quiet poetry of untouched heart-spaces, where you are in contact with a fullness beyond words. The gift from the other fulfils an inexpressible longing of your life. To be loved is always a surprise.

DHL: It is both liberating and disturbing. Nothing has prepared you for this mixture of flow and fragility. You are transformed, graced, religious in its deepest sense.

JA: You are open not just to the other person but to the call of life beyond your little self. When people discover love born between them, they are invited, in a real sense, towards God.

DHL: They are taken out of their lonely ego worlds, to join not just a duet of intimacy but a symphony of full life.

JA: You see, our languages are different, but we celebrate the same human release from falsity into freedom.

DHL: From oppression into joy, and that joy is a gateway towards God.

JA: Without it we live as shadows of ourselves.

DHL: With it we enter kingdoms of energy.

JA: But if our words soar too high, we forget that love takes flesh in the ordinary.

DHL: It takes flesh in flesh, which is extraordinary and ordinary together.

REFLECTION SPACE

The Scottish philosopher John Macmurray was a constant explorer of the centrality of personal friendship. Here are some snippets of his thought.

From *The Self as Agent*:

> Personal existence is constituted by the relation of persons.
> All meaningful knowledge is for the sake of action, and all meaningful action for the sake of friendship.
> The cultural crisis of our time is a crisis of the personal.
> The Self cannot exist in isolation.

From *Reason and Emotion*:

> I am prepared to bank upon the faith that the essence of nature – human and divine – is love.
> The personal life is essentially a life of relations between people; to be ourselves at all we need other people.
> Religion grows out of our relation to persons.

According to Sebastian Moore, 'the essential mystery of the person' has a double source: each person is 'unique and of absolute value' and yet 'has his/her flourishing in the power of another'. Paradoxically when 'we try to give a full description of a person's existence we find ourselves talking about two persons!'

Each friend represents a world in us, a world possibly not
born until they arrive.

(Anais Nin)

Nobody came today, nobody,
and I have died so little in my life.

(from Kevin Hart's poem 'Agape')

In J. M. Synge's masterpiece *The Playboy of the Western World*, a
significant moment comes when Pegeen has discovered the
eloquence of love and comments on her transformation from her
previously sarcastic self:

'And to think it's me is talking sweetly, and I the fright of
seven townlands for my biting tongue. Well, the heart's a
wonder.'

CHAPTER 3

STRUGGLES AND SHADOWS

Everything you deny simply accumulates. Let your wound stay open. Then from the depth of your night a humbler joy can be born.

(Jean Sulivan)

To stand in Auschwitz is to have your backbone turned into a question mark about the nature of the human being.

(John Moriarty)

This chapter looks at an area of experience that we are shy about. We carry hurts and guilts of so many kinds – usually wrapped in silence. And yet owning of our vulnerability is not only a way to spiritual transparency, as the wisdom of all religions testify. It is also a crucial step towards gentler aliveness as human beings together. Many imaginative writers have the courage to force us to enter these self-wounded zones.

DISTURBING UNDERWORLDS

Eyes Wide Shut, Stanley Kubrick's controversial last film, is a contemporary example of diving deeper. It portrays a rich New York couple who live on the surface of themselves. In the opening moments between husband and wife come two simple but significant questions: 'Honey, have you seen my wallet?' and 'How do I look?' They seem to sum up a high society reduced to appearances and money. The first signs that there is trouble underneath all the sophistication come when, under the influence of marijuana, they dip into ambiguous zones of fantasy and mutual suspicion that they would normally avoid. After crossing this initial threshold the story becomes more frightening. Jealousy and distrust take over. Both of them descend into underworlds of sexual dreaming and drifting. They undergo a peeling away of smugness and an exposure to unexpected vulnerability. They discover that they have been living behind masks or through images in mirrors (key symbols within the film). They wake up to rivers of uncertainty and darkness flowing behind the façade of their normality.

A constantly repeated question is 'Are you sure?' Gradually the film becomes an initiation into fear, accompanied by menacing notes on the piano. In this way also the film's audience is forced to recognise the fragility of our certainties and the corruption of a world where wealth can buy anything and where power can conceal its crimes. But there are also sources of salvation at work. In Bill (Tom Cruise) there is a natural generosity, especially in his work as a doctor. In Alice (Nicole Kidman) an intuitive courage pushes her to voice her temptations to infidelity. In the night world that Bill enters, he finds prostitutes who display kindness and one who saves his life (earlier, as a doctor, he had helped to save hers). In this nocturnal world the rationality of common sense breaks down. But only after this Dante-like visit to the underworld can the couple arrive at a humbled honesty and a tentative renewal of their relationship. After her father's death, Kubrick's daughter indicated an intended theme of the film: 'If you think there is no evil in you, you've not looked hard enough.' In Eyes Wide Shut this evil is unmasked both within the self and within the whole social system.

These undermining journeys take place in the period before Christmas. There are Christmas trees in every place except the palace of decadence where Bill nearly loses his life. Most of these trees are artificial, suggesting a society of empty signs where Christmas becomes a commercial orgy. Yet into this world of falsity come hints of healing. In their final conversation, as they wander through a luxury store filled with Christmas toys, Bill asks Alice what they should do, now that their lives have been shaken out of their complacency, because *'no dream is just a dream.'* She replies hesitantly. *'Maybe, I think, we should be grateful . . . grateful that we've managed to survive through all of our adventures, whether they were real or only a dream.'* Even the repetition of 'grateful' points to a tone of humility and forgiveness. The end remains ambiguous. Have they had their eyes opened wider to the brittle beauty of any deep relationship? Have they realised how easily what is precious can be damaged by insensitivity or eroded by the drifting culture around them? As in much of his previous work, Kubrick's tone is akin to a biblical prophet, austere, demanding and disturbing.

This powerful if not always convincing film reveals a pattern typical of our human struggles. There are moments when each of us runs into destructive demons, and such encounters can leave us feeling shaken or fragile. Then either we retreat into normality or else we have courage to face more humbling revelations. Any love relationship will sooner or later touch zones of vulnerability. How do I cope with the strangeness of the other person, or with the hurts that happen even unconsciously? Or with volcanoes that erupt at times of intensity? The typical temptation is to forget the subversive shadows I have glimpsed: they were merely imagination. But when I risk staying in touch with my weakness or fear, and even more so, if I can communicate what I feel to another person, shadows become thresholds of transformation. Then I move closer to what the gospel calls 'poverty of spirit', or to the openness of the 'child'. It is the ancient wisdom of a *felix culpa*, a fall into guilt that opens doors, forcing me to seek help, human and divine. Or, in the subtle metaphor of a George Herbert poem, God works a 'pulley': what on one side weighs down, paradoxically raises up on the other side.

THE SECRET OF OUR HEARTS

Some 160 years before Kubrick, John Henry Newman, as an Anglican minister, preached an unusual sermon around Christmas, in which he spoke of avoidance of our human 'wounds' as *the* reason why our religious beliefs remain 'so unreal'. 'We have each the same secret, and we keep it to our-selves, and we fear that, as a cause of estrangement, which really would be a bond of union.' Newman saw this fear of facing our shadows as the root of our shallowness. Because 'we dare not trust each other with the secret of our hearts' – our sense of failure and resultant vulnerability – 'our love is not enlarged' and 'our religion, viewed as a social system, is hollow'. The title Newman gave to his sermon was 'Christian Sympathy', with the implication that if God embraces all human woundedness in Christ, we too are invited into a surprising lowering of our defences.

That text is extraordinary for its time. It talks about a possibility of staying on the surface both of life and of faith. This fear leaves us unable to trust anyone with the dim corners that lurk in every life. These unvoiced burdens, according to Newman, leave us unfree to live fully. And these silences, when shared, create hollowness within what passes for religion.

My own experience can verify the intuition that unites Newman and Kubrick. During my years as a lecturer in litera-ture I was often an unofficial counsellor for students. Again and again when exam time was approaching, I used think to myself, 'There won't be much to do these days on the personal level: any contacts will be about study'. And I was always wrong. Students often knocked on the door to mention some worry about the exams. But it was only an excuse. The real agenda was else-where, and usually, it has something to do with negative areas of their personal experience.

Why did exam time bring these feelings to the fore? I have no clear answer. Perhaps the pressure of study, and the solitude involved, forced them to listen to themselves more than in the normal run of things. All I know is that my listening skills were kept busy in those weeks. And it was nearly always a question of voicing some previously unvoiced 'secret'. Its forms were many. It could be some sense of shame over a family situation, or a self-doubt about sexuality, or a relationship that went wrong, or simply the worries caused by ordinary egoism. I felt blessed to be able to offer a safe space of honesty, and to witness a healing born from that courage to trust. If destructiveness stems from unlived life (as Erik Fromm said), Newman and Kubrick offer another light: our guilts can become numb self-hatred when they cannot find expression. But, more positively, some voicing of difficult truth can create new self-attitudes. When the magnifying glass of loneliness is broken, burdens become more liveable, and often the road is opened towards the listening that leads to faith.

As Newman and Kubrick imply, it can be strangely difficult to find the space to voice fears and shadows. It is the area that religion calls sin and it is commonplace in church circles today to lament a loss of a 'sense of sin'. The trouble is that most of the Church's sin-talk has lost its roots in human experience. It comes across as moralistic and not 'real' (both in Newman's sense as personally involving and as in the contemporary phrase 'get real'). And yet the human reality of refusal and evil exists. It would be a trivialisation of our self-images to lose touch with the sources of our unease, with feelings of exile or moral impotence. Imaginative writers have preserved a powerful honesty about these underworlds of our experience. As Alexander Solzhenitsyn once remarked, literature does not exist to put make-up on the face of humanity but rather to face the scars. It reminds us constantly that we need release from oppressions of many kinds, and that our freedom path is slow and costly.

DISMANTLING THE SHIELDS

> In guilt the other is experienced not as presence but as
> pressure.
>
> (Sebastian Moore)

One of the masterpieces of religious fiction is *The Diary of a
Country Priest* by Georges Bernanos. First published in 1936, it
was made into an austere film directed by Bresson. It tells the
story of a young priest in a village in France, a peasant figure
of failure and inadequacy – at least in his own eyes – who
nevertheless serves his people with dedication and his own kind
of wisdom. A central scene in the novel involves a long conversation between this unnamed curate and the Countess. It
is one of the most gripping embodiments of conversion of heart
in all literature. Bernanos was to write in his own diary in 1948,
'sin has no depth, it keeps us living on the surface of ourselves,
but God awaits us within, if only we would enter to find
nourishment'.

The Countess is someone locked into hate for God and for life,
and unable to rediscover her other feelings. She has managed to
hide her vulnerability from everyone and even from herself,
until this unexpected conversation with the priest, when she
voices her dark truth for the first time in her life. Everything
hinges on the tragic death of her only son many years previously, and on how her husband and her daughter had made her life
one of lonely torment and betrayal. This encounter brings her
face to face with her 'frozen heart' and allows her to emerge from
long years 'in that horrible and silent space of desolation'. The
brilliant delicacy of this conversation shows how imaginative
writing may evoke underworlds – and salvation from them –
with a power beyond the reach of most religious discourse.

After the Countess is provoked into revealing her desire that
her daughter might remain similarly locked up in her pride, the
priest says, 'Madame, one gets used to not loving . . . blessed

would be the sins that opened doors of shame for you'. A little later with an edge of anger he says, 'God will break you'.

'God has broken me already,' she replied. 'He took my son. I no longer fear Him.' And she admits, 'I hate Him'.

'Your closed heart may separate you from your son for all eternity . . . hell means to stop loving, to stop understanding, and yet to live.'

As if he had gone too far because of his desire to help her, and feeling himself lost and out of his depth in this confrontation, the priest begins to weep gently. This solidarity with her pain begins to thaw her 'savage sulkiness' and 'rebellion'. Gently she recounts to him the death of her little boy. The priest, almost by accident, has found a chink in her armour where light can enter.

'She was trembling now. I seemed to be standing there alone between God and this tortured human being.'

The priest dares to speak to her of Christ: 'You know that our God came to be among us.' Clutching the medallion of her dead son, the Countess asks him to repeat what he had said earlier about hell.

'Hell is not to love any more. As long as we remain in this life we can still deceive ourselves, imagining that we love by our own strength, that we can love without God. But we are like madmen stretching out our hands to grasp the moon mirrored in water. I'm sorry. I express it so badly.'

The scene ends with the Countess praying the Our Father, even though she resists the words 'Thy will be done on earth'. He tells her to surrender everything to God, her sorrows and even her pride.

And she says with surprising honesty to the priest, 'an hour ago my life was perfectly in control . . . you've left nothing standing'.

'God wants us to be merciful with ourselves,' he tells her. She kneels for his blessing and his prayer for her peace.

That evening he receives a letter from her. 'I have lived in the most terrible loneliness . . . I am not resigned. I'm happy. I don't want anything . . . I hope again.' And a few hours later she died.

Bernanos strips away her masks of pride only to bring her to a recovery of joy.

This dialogue encounter between priest and Countess takes up some twenty-five pages in the novel. Yet even this outline conveys the struggle of acknowledging deep wounds and the humility that can bring healing. We get hurt. We become hard. We remain stuck in some negativity. We stop imagining any change for ourselves. The closure space comes to seem normal. We desperately need someone to act as a mirror of our self-punishment. A mirror uniting compassion and challenge. Out of the sacrament of another person's companionship, and their courage to visit our underworlds with us, we arrive at a new life-tone, where all the great religious words take flesh again: forgiveness, humility, faith, hope, love, peace . . . But without some human journey into honesty, often the religious one will lack roots and staying power.

CONFRONTING OUR PETTINESS

'Snake', one of the most celebrated poems of D. H. Lawrence, focuses on an episode that exposed his own smallness of spirit. It describes how a snake came to the well in his garden on a hot July day in Sicily.

> Someone was before me at my water-trough,
> And I, like a second-comer, waiting.
> He lifted his head from his drinking, as cattle do,
> And looked at me vaguely, as drinking cattle do . . .

This presence provokes an inner conflict in the poet. The 'voices of his education' tell him to kill it as dangerous. But intuitively he likes him and wants to welcome him as a guest.

> Was it cowardice, that I dared not kill him?
> Was it perversity, that I longed to talk to him?
> Was it humility, to feel so honoured?

When the snake starts to climb the wall to leave, without clear motive the poet impulsively picks up a log and throws it at the water-trough, perhaps without hitting the snake, who disappears into a dark hole.

> And immediately I regretted it.
> I thought how paltry, how vulgar, what a mean act! . . .
> For he seemed to me again like a king,
> Like a king in exile, uncrowned in the underworld . . .
> And so, I missed my chance with one of the lords
> Of life.
> And I have something to expiate:
> A pettiness.

The poem hinges on a conflict between desires. Common sense says that snakes should be killed or at least chased away. But the snake awakens another level of wonder and reverence. Some might call it the unconscious or primitive in each of us. When the dominant culture wins and the log is hurled, there is an experience of remorse or self-disgust. It seems a fall from grace that requires some atonement. Like the famous killing of the albatross in Coleridge's 'The Rime of the Ancient Mariner', 'Snake' offers a symbolic moment of guilt over a trivial act of fear, not of obvious evil, but of self-damaging 'pettiness'. Not all failures and refusals are dramatic.

THRESHOLDS OF TENDERNESS

I take a final and more positive example from an Irish play that had huge international success in the mid 1990s. Sebastian Barry's *The Steward of Christendom* depicts the retired head of the Dublin city police, now in a home for the elderly. He is a difficult old man, solitary and moody. As he looks back on his life, he recalls episodes that have shaped him. One of these occurs as a magnificent monologue at the end of the First Act. It captures a key moment when he abandoned his authoritarian façade and discovered unexpected gentleness. As one commentator has said: Sebastian Barry's central characters are 'in the religious sense, full of grace, touched by some kind of inexplicable tenderness that grants them an equivocal but unmistakable blessing'.

In this long speech Thomas recounts how he was so jittery during his wife's labour in giving birth to their youngest child Dolly that the midwife told him to go outside for a walk near the sea. He does so and begins to think back on their marriage, on how the children depended so much on their mother and 'how stupid and silent I was', especially with his only son.

'I started to tremble, it was a moment in your life when daily things pass away from you, when all your concerns seem to vanish, and you are allowed by God a little space of clarity and grace. When you see that God himself is in your wife and in your children, and they hold in trust for you your own measure of goodness. And in the manner of your treatment of them lies your own salvation.'

Thomas returns to the house 'a simpler man than the one who had set out'. As he holds his new-born daughter, he pledges all 'my heart and life to that face . . . all the usefulness of my days to that face'.

It is a significant moment of transformation, when the stern and role-bound policeman finds another language within himself. It is another example of exodus from self-woundedness, less agonised than in the stories of Kubrick or Bernanos, but celebrating the human capacity to escape from prisons and to receive (or create) new self-images to live by.

DIALOGUE OF DIFFERENT HORIZONS

I have faith in the working-out of higher possibilities than the Catholic or any other church has presented . . . to do without opium and live through all our pain with conscious clear-eyed endurance.

(George Eliot)

Redemption is meaningless unless there is cause for it in the actual life we live, and for the last few centuries there has been operating in our culture the secular belief that there is no such cause.

(Flannery O'Connor)

The following imaginary conversation brings together two great writers of fiction. Flannery O'Connor died of lupus in 1964 before she reached the age of forty, whereas a century earlier George Eliot (in reality Marian Evans) only began to publish fiction in her late thirties. O'Connor was a convinced Catholic and arguably the most theologically knowledgeable among imaginative writers of this last century. Eliot was also highly literate in theology although she lost her Christian faith in her early twenties. Having been unusually pious and puritan in her outlook, her religious certainties crumbed under an avalanche of doubts about the historical truth of the Bible. She went on to become the translator of Feuerbach's masterpiece of atheism into English (her version of *The Essence of Christianity* is still on sale). Under his influence she decided that human beings imagined God as a crutch or source of comfort in a frightening world. After several years of intellectual work, she turned to the writing of fiction with something of a religious passion. She saw her contemporaries as 'yearning for a faith that will harmonise' aspiration and new knowledge. In this spirit her novels embody a philosophy of 'higher sympathy', exploring how people move from 'unreflecting egoism' towards 'living, generous humanity'. Life, for her, was 'not a struggle to submit' but 'a struggle to accept with passion and with joy'.

Flannery O'Connor, by contrast, specialised in ironic stories where her characters are brought face to face with their attitudes of refusal and jerked into something like humility. Her tone is tough rather than pious and her plots usually hinge on a stormy conversion of disposition. She was refreshingly blunt about her religious stance. Her stories concentrate on 'the violences which precede and follow' the intrusions of grace in people's lives. 'My audience', she wrote, 'are the people who think God is dead', and her intuition was that through comedy some of the withered roots of religious imagination could be coaxed back into life. She thought that American culture was kidnapped by a dangerous superficiality, and, with characteristic verve, she commented that the funeral of President Kennedy was 'a salutary tonic for this back-slapping gum chewing hiya-kid nation'. Through her stories she wanted to pierce this flimsy screen against darker truth or, in contemporary language, to 'deconstruct' the smugness of her characters. In this she has much in common with her non-believing nineteenth-century interlocutor. Eliot in turn would surely agree with O'Connor's claim that 'the basic experience of everyone is the experience of human limitation'.

With such differences on religious matters and such convergences in their sense of the human drama, we can imagine these two authors in conversation about human vulnerability and about the various strategies we use to avoid admitting our wounds. Sentences in italics are almost exact quotations.

Disturbing the illusions

Flannery: You have an elaborate metaphor in *Middlemarch* that I always liked. It goes like this. *'If we had a keen vision and feeling of all ordinary human life, it would be like hearing the grass grow and the squirrel's heart beat, and we should die of that roar which lies on the other side of silence. As it is, the quickest of us walk about well-wadded with stupidity.'*

I know we interpret life differently but on that last point we are agreed: people can walk around unconscious of the battlements they build to protect their egoism. We both believed in shattering those illusions.

George: To return the compliment, what I admire in your fiction is your comic approach to those 'well-wadded' characters.

You expose their cover. You make them have some crash of their self-images. Perhaps your most famous line was in the mouth of the murderer of an obstinate old grandmother: *'She would have been a good woman if there had been somebody there to shoot her every minute of her life'*! She stopped playing her games of power only in the instant when she knew she could die.

F: I wanted to put her in touch with her *essential poverty*. Often some loss of their security is necessary to jolt us.

G: We stop running from our fragility.

F: Or more dangerously from our self-lies.

G: But nobody likes to visit the underworld within themselves.

F: For me the dark that we avoid is our pride. We cunningly protect ourselves from having our complacency upset. In fact sin is surprisingly conservative – it means refusing to grow.

G: What you call pride, I see as blindness. The surrounding world keeps us on the surface of ourselves. We become like sleepwalkers until some small incident triggers our suspicion.

F: For me Christian faith fulfils us by dismantling us in unwelcome ways.

G: Even on a human level we are afraid to love. We fear its price. Therefore we compromise and look for a cheaper way to live.

F: I enjoyed leading my characters towards an experience of impotence. I pictured them as addicted to a controlled life, where everything was in place. They had constructed defence systems against any real change. They were the centre of their universe and they were always comically right. I relished the build-up to the shock that shattered their self-world. Can we ever be changed by grace *without a blasting annihilating light, a blast that will last a lifetime*? Grace is not always gentle. It has to be rough to get through the fortifications.

Selfishness or sin?

G: We are both talking about 'pride and prejudice' and about its crumbling into something of new 'sense and sensibility' (to borrow from our colleague Jane!). But 'grace' is something I'm not sure of.

F: You explore egoism without calling it sin. It's the same human reality but 'sin' means a different interpretation of our human darkness. We see ourselves with God's eyes, so to speak. The surprising thing is that we are so wrong about sin. Once recognised it can be our springboard into new life, not just a source of self-guilt.

G: Something is terribly wrong or missing in our lives, no matter what you call it. The journey of my characters is from the closed ego into what I call 'sympathy'. It shows in a reaching out to the weaker in this world, and in a new sense of one's own fragility. Is it not similar to your springboard from sin into grace?

F: With this major difference: your journey is all within the self; mine starts within but is surprised into relationship. Your road seems too lonely. My road involves God, the ultimate unLonely One, who liberates us not only from our pride but from the illusion of being so alone.

G: That was my faith when I was young. My sense of a need for change of heart stayed with me but I could no longer see that we were anything but alone in this world. But I know that I have lost a great vision that held everything more richly together.

F: Allowing for that divergence, let's come back to experiences of failure. Is there something in us that can best be liberated by an experience of vulnerability?

G: We live with smallness, to the point of self-deception. We can imprison ourselves without knowing it. Along comes some negative self-revelation that shakes our sandcastles. In this way failure can become a source of energy.

F: 'Revelation' is the title of one of my last stories, written when I was dying. My Mrs Turpin had to be shocked by seeing her twisted self before she could open up to the greatness of God's mercy. She was so self-satisfied as a Christian that she was comically blind to her lack of compassion. Everything goes wrong for her. A disturbed girl calls her a 'wart hog' from hell!

This one terrible day fuels her rage against God and eventually she roars at God *'Who do you think you are!'* But the question comes back to her as an echo, as an answer!

G: That's a good moment. I have to ask that question but I don't imagine myself being asked by God. So Mrs Turpin finds grace?

F: She sees her life with humbler eyes. Salvation can only make sense when our woundedness has come into focus. In fact Christ's most frequent action was to heal.

Achievement or gift?

G: I agree that people fall into half-life. And they have to recognise their cages before they open to 'sympathy' or 'grace'. I know there are worlds of difference between those two words. Sympathy for me is a human achievement. Grace for you is a divine gift.

F: Grace undermines the sense that our lives are simply our 'achievement'. I am happily traditional. I hold that *evil is the wrong use of good and that without grace we get it wrong most of the time.*

G: That is one major difference between us but there is another. We agree that people have to be rescued from various forms of paralysis. You see it as self-induced woundedness. I see many people as damaged by their experience of life. They are more victims than agents. If they are closed or selfish, it comes from what happened to them rather than from choice. Disappointment more than decision accounts for a lot of human pain.

F: My closed characters are not victims of circumstance. They had shaped themselves that way, gradually but freely. They thought that the only way to cope with life was to look after 'number one'. So I see them as responsible for their own prisons. I wanted to make serious fun of their slow self-destruction.

G: I recognise the possibility of a self-chosen egoism. I am drawn to explore situations that kill the imagination. How can life return to someone whose confidence has been dented?

F: I was more theological and you were more humanist. I wanted to make people vulnerable to their need for salvation. You invited your readers to glimpse the pain of the wounded from within, which is certainly another face of vulnerability.

G: Even when I lost my faith in God, I did not lose the sense of compassion that I had learned from the gospels. I treasure the moments when we get in touch with the 'child' in us. *Generosity in others can change the lights for us.*

F: For me it is God's Spirit, through self-failure, or through that goodness of others, who dismantles our protective shields.

G: The beauty of that old vision has been destroyed for me. The new questions make it impossible to say a simple yes.

F: Either there is a gift of light that changes everything, or else we are on our own, self-creating, and condemned to frustration. Unless I can discover that my life is shattered joyfully by a huge love.

G: By human love, shadowed by struggle, yes. By Love eternal, I simply don't know.

REFLECTION SPACE

The literal meaning of *hamartia*, the Greek word for sin in the New Testament, is 'missing the mark', as in archery. Have we worthy wavelengths for facing the ways in which we fall short of the target of fullness of life? Have we wisdom to visit the darkness?

> To be salvific, the experience of chaos, that is the radical breakdown of the predictable, must be openly acknowledged; we cannot learn from this ordeal if we deny it is happening to us. This is what we mean by conversion in Gospel life.

> (Gerald Arbuckle)

Again Sebastian Moore offers some original angles:

Human living as it is normally pursued is an escape from reality. The gospel message is a recall to reality, revealed as a mystery of forgiveness.

(*God Is a New Language*)

It takes considerable schooling in self-understanding to discover the 'to hell with everything but me' that underlies the most innocent attitudes and actions.

You prefer not to face the full situation, which is that you have hurt another person by shrinking yourself. When you hurt another person, your true self, the lover in you, goes into hiding, and uses every possible ruse to stay in hiding. Even abject apology!

(*The Crucified Is No Stranger*)

Wounded we cross the desert's emptiness
and must be false to what would make us whole,
For only change and distance shape for us
Some new tremendous symbol for the soul.

(From Judith Wright, *Five Senses*)

CHAPTER 4

CRIES OF TRAGEDY

Freedom literally comes from having our self-absorption challenged by the needs of another.

(Stanley Hauerwas)

Others have a cross to carry and we realize we cannot take it from them. It is harder than carrying one's own.

(Edith Stein)

The previous section looked at personal versions of egoism or sin. There remains the larger world of pain that is human history. To acknowledge one's own spirit of refusal is a step towards freedom and even towards faith. To be truly present to the suffering of others, whether of individuals close to us or to the many poor victims around, is a different avenue towards transformation.

Sometimes that journey starts with an embarrassing revelation. In late 2000 I spent several weeks teaching in Nairobi. It was my first real exposure to Africa, and it was both a happy and a disturbing experience. Happy because of the tangible aliveness of people, shown in so many ways from hospitality to celebration. Disturbing because of the presence of poverty and pain in so many forms: the thousands of street children; villages with grandparents and children – the middle generation destroyed

by AIDS. On the day I arrived an American priest was murdered, probably because he was too critical of the government.
The shadows are long and many.

My 'embarrassing revelation' happened about halfway
through my stay. I developed a septic toe. What could be more
petty? My hosts insisted that I see a doctor. He prescribed a
familiar brand of antibiotics but when I went to the pharmacy to
get them, I had not enough money. They cost twice as much as
back home, and I had to borrow money from a friend who had
come with me. How, I asked him, could people pay such high
prices for imported medicine? 'They can't even think of buying
them,' he replied. 'Your tablets would be three weeks' wages for
an unskilled worker.' I started to take the tablets for my sore toe,
but with a humbling sense of guilt. I had glimpsed, once again,
the contrast between my cushioned life and the daily situation
for millions.

By coincidence the newspaper of the next day carried a list of
prices for a 'Big Mac' in various cities throughout the world. In
London, New York or Tokyo, you can earn the local price of a
burger with less than twenty minutes' work. In Nairobi, you
would have to work for three hours to buy the same sandwich.
Another small summary of something hugely wrong.

Widen the picture. Take the news of any given day. So many
disasters, small or large. Rivalry lurks everywhere. Hatreds
explode. Violence reigns. Corruption corrodes. Something terrible goes wrong when we have no goal but ourselves. I
remember standing on the platform of a suburban station in
England on a Saturday afternoon. Few people were around.
Suddenly the place filled up with young men in bad humour,
fans of a defeated football team, with shaved heads, beer cans,
and heavy boots. Rightly or wrongly I felt afraid. I imagined
that any false move on my part would provoke an attack; if I
even opened the book I was carrying. The ugliness of humanity
emerges in many ways. That railway platform was a minor
glimpse of 'the horror, the horror'.

Those famous words come from Joseph Conrad's short novel

Heart of Darkness, which tells of a nightmare journey into what humankind can become in 'utter solitude without a policeman'. It predates the comment of Henri de Lubac that humanity without God sooner or later becomes anti-human. Conrad's masterpiece of pessimism is set in the late nineteenth century, the high era of commercial imperialism, when a certain Kurtz went into the jungles of Africa to search for ivory. The narrator of the tale, Marlow, is sent up river to find Kurtz, only to uncover a situation of terrifying depravity and insanity. The details are all the more frightening because they are left deliberately vague. The 'principles' of civilization are exposed as 'rags that would fly off at the first good shake'. Kurtz had set himself up as a kind of dictator 'satiated with primitive emotions'. In Marlow's words 'I saw on that ivory face the expression of sombre pride, of ruthless power, of craven terror – of an intense and hopeless despair'. Kurtz dies in Marlow's presence crying out 'The horror, the horror'.

Back in Europe Marlow is a changed man, burdened by the appalling evil he had encountered in the jungle. He meets the dead man's fiancée who wants only to nourish her ideal picture of Kurtz.

> 'His last word – to live with,' she insisted. 'Don't you understand I loved him – I loved him – I loved him!'
> I pulled myself together and spoke slowly.
> 'The last word he pronounced was – your name.'
> I heard a light sigh and then my heart stood still, stopped dead short by an exulting and terrible cry, by the cry of inconceivable triumph and of unspeakable pain. 'I knew it – I was sure!' She knew. She was sure . . . I could not tell her. It would have been too dark – too dark altogether.

Thus *Heart of Darkness* ends with a moment of frightening irony: the glimpse into the underside of history is compounded by the cowardice of a lie. Darkness exists but we are not able to face it. Indeed, there may be a more subtle twist at the end. Could Marlow possibly be telling the truth? The rich European lady is, in a sense, 'the horror'. With her false imagining of the world she summarises an elegant evasion of evil. To adapt an intuition of Walter Benjamin, the victory arches of ancient Rome are tombstones over the graves of forgotten victims.

If Conrad's overwhelmingly negative view of darkness were the only approach available to the evils around, we would be left without much hope. There is a sense in which Conrad, and many great nihilists like him, remained paralysed before the terrible facts of tragedy. To repeat a key image of this book, they seem unable to cross a threshold into a different imagination of evil. In each of our zones of human searching there comes a crisis: either one goes towards a costly conversion or one remains stuck with inherited responses before the challenges of life. As against the numb eloquence of a Conrad there are all the prophetic voices that confront evil and suffering in a different tone. Without denying or fleeing from 'the imagination of disaster' (a phrase from Henry James), they manage to forge an alternative stance before 'the horror'. Religious faith changes the horizon without denying the reality of darkness. Where Conrad concentrated on the twisted mind of an oppressor, a religious sensibility will want to listen also to the voices of the victims.

THE REBELLION OF JOB

The tragic symbols speak in the silence of the humiliated ethical.

(Paul Ricoeur)

In this regard the greatest pre-Christian story is undoubtedly the Book of Job. As a biblical text it is unique: it makes no mention of such themes as covenant or temple or exodus, and the principal characters come from outside the Jewish tradition. It is a poetic tale that undermines and mocks all stock responses to suffering. It is enough to recall that the initial parable starts with a wager between God and the Accuser (the meaning of 'Satan', not to be confused with the devil). God bets on Job's fidelity in spite of any possible disaster. In his sardonic way Satan holds that religion is grounded in a profit motive, in the sense of a quest for security. If you take away the props, disinterested faith cannot survive. Such cynicism is wrong, says God. And ultimately – after much torment and conflict – God wins the bet placed on humanity. Authentic faith can survive terrible storms and deserts and can purify itself in the process.

A central theme of the book lies in the contrast between Job's complaints and the guilt theories espoused by his 'friends' to interpret his afflictions. They come with genuine sympathy to be with him in his distress but after sitting with him in silence for a week, they try to explain everything and advise him on his response. Here their words flounder. Their commonplace responses ring false, whereas his vehement cries ring true. They talk 'theology' in the worst sense. They proclaim certainties. They tell the tortured man that he must have deserved it. Job, by contrast, cries out from the chaos of his experience. His agonised speeches are a chorus of 'why?' Behind their speeches lies an insulting image both of humanity and of divinity. Human beings, it would seem, are corrupt and deny the extent of their twistedness. Their God is a wily manager who knows how to punish such falsity and hidden sin. But Job rejects this school of retribution as simply 'the left-overs of infidelity' (21:34).

In this way the book dramatises not just the suffering of a good person, but also the yawning gap between the experience of tragedy and the God-images available. The poem gives voice to the embittered lamentations of Job, and at the same time satirises the hollowness of a religion of bargaining over rewards and punishments. Its central question concerns what kind of God is credible in a world where such suffering strikes. Job, in spite of all the desolation he feels, manages not to 'curse God and die' (the advice of his wife at the outset); 'my lips will never speak evil' he claims (27:4), insisting that all his life he had lived with compassion as 'eyes for the blind, feet for the lame, father of the poor' (29:15–16).

One of Job's demands is to meet God in order to get divine answers to the issues so poorly dealt with by his friends. In words made famous through Handel's *Messiah*, Job expresses his trust: 'I know that my Redeemer lives and in my flesh I shall see God' (19:25–26). This hope is to come true in an unexpected way. God eventually speaks 'from the heart of the tempest', but not as a philosopher on the problem of pain. Nothing is said about suffering or about innocence or guilt. The issue of 'why' gives way to the issue of 'who' God is. A series of questions reveals the smallness of Job's horizon and the differentness of God: 'Have you been shown the gates of Death . . . or visited the place where the snow is stored?' Job can only respond that his words have been unworthy and that he has no more to say. His imagination of God has set itself free from models of human justice. In the insightful words of G. K. Chesterton,

> A more trivial poet would have made God enter in order to answer the questions . . . In this drama of scepticism God Himself takes up the role of sceptic. He asks of Job the question that any criminal accused by Job would be most entitled to ask. He asks Job who he is. And Job . . . comes to the conclusion that he does not know.

This ancient masterpiece on suffering shifts the debate forever from a seeking-of-answers for the mind towards a sense-of-presence for the spirit. The friends are rebuked by God. Job had fallen into their level of thinking by imagining God in a merely human way – as if God 'should' reward his goodness. Answers on that level are impossible. The only real 'answer' lies in the relationship to the Mystery of Love that – in spite of all his trials – Job had never doubted. Thus the healing moment comes not through what God says but through the transforming presence of God. This is a logic of gift, not of exchange. The otherness and distance of God remains, but Job now realises that a huge intimacy embraces his life. He sees through his 'ignorant words' and ends with a cry of wonder:

Before, I knew you only by hearsay
But now I have seen you with my own eyes. (42:5)

As Chesterton put it, interrogation is replaced by exclamation. The horizon of the victim is not the only one. The least inadequate 'answer' to tragedy comes from a new depth of experience, a new perspective. It lies in the realm, not of explanations, but of encounter, where debating gives way to another threshold, one of mutual relationship across the gulf of mystery. After all his wrestling, Job's image of God is altered. His trust has survived the dark. At dawn he discovers the majesty of God and that trust is a two-way flow. God has become both utterly beyond and amazingly near. Job has been carried, so to speak, across a threshold where his friends, and so many of us, remain stuck. His story is one of the classics of diving deeper.

CHRISTIAN SENSE OF TRAGEDY

My heart is moved by all I cannot save:
So much has been destroyed.

(Adrienne Rich)

Oscar Romero, Archbishop of San Salvador, was killed while saying Mass on 24 March 1980. The previous day he had ended his Sunday sermon, broadcast on radio, with an appeal to the soldiers involved in attacks on the poor: 'I order you in the name of God: stop this repression.' In his three short years as archbishop he emerged from obscurity and became a prophetic figure of courage on the world stage. In fact the man who had been chosen as archbishop because of his caution and conservatism had undergone a deep conversion. Faced with the suffering of ordinary people, he found his own faith being challenged into action. 'It is not hard,' he remarked, 'to be a good shepherd for such people.' In 1977 he had an insight that proved a turning point in his life: 'when the world around us is founded on an established disorder, the proclamation of the Gospel becomes subversive.' Gradually he became a voice for the voiceless, increasingly vehement in his denunciations of the violent tactics of the military against the poor.

In his diary during the months before his death he wrote: 'Our faith is enlarged and the mysteries we believe become deeper, when we take seriously the option for the poor.' 'Faith which is lived out in isolation from life is not true faith.' A few weeks before being killed he did a retreat and jotted down in his note-book that 'a violent death in these circumstances is quite poss-ible', adding that it takes more courage to surrender one's life to God than to face death. Only twelve days before his assassin-ation he wrote: 'the gospel becomes a source of conflict when it stops being a nice theory and when we try to live it.'

Clearly the Romero of the following conversation is a creation based on reality and this is even more true of his interlocutor, 'Shakespeare'. Of the real William Shakespeare we know merci-fully little, and what we know tells us next to nothing of his philosophy of life. Romero became a contemporary symbol of how faith can confront huge social suffering. Shakespeare too is a symbolic figure who explored human agony and evil especial-ly through his tragedies. His imagination is obviously Christian even if his explicit Christian references are few. As distinct from the great Greek tragedies, Shakespeare believes in human free-dom rather than in preordained fate. In ways unthinkable for the ancient world, his tragedies move beyond disaster into glimpses of reconciliation and transcendence in his main characters and equally in the experience of his audience.

Perhaps it is only Christian cultures that move towards tragedy as potential transformation. A simple and eloquent example of this sensibility comes in the dedication that Eugene O'Neill gave to his great modern tragedy *A Long Day's Journey into Night*. It is a largely autobiographical play recalling the mutually inflicted pain within a family. Dedicating it to his wife, O'Neill wrote that her love and tenderness had given him 'the faith in love that enabled me to face my dead at last and write this play – write it with deep pity and understanding and forgiveness for all the four haunted Tyrones'. No Greek dramatist of ancient times could have written those words. To face horrors was fated for them. For Conrad it was merely traumatic and petrifying. For tragedy in a Christian horizon, the amazing possibility is to be able to move through the horror towards another plane of tenderness and towards something of forgiveness.

DRAMATIST AND ARCHBISHOP

Let us imagine Shakespeare and Romero in the middle of a conversation about suffering and about witnessing the pain of others . . .

Facing the obscenity

S: I wrote tragedies to explore unvisited zones of life, those that we prefer to forget when life is tranquil.

R: We not only forget. We avoid the suffering of others unless it forces itself on our attention.

S: We pretend not to hear the cries, because we can't cope with such immensity.

R: The cry of the poor has become the new obscenity – literally what is not allowed on to the stage. In older times sex was banned. Now the suffering of people is censored or sentimentalised.

S: But surely the presence of tragedy changes our attitudes. It can reveal our smallness.

R: Attitudes can be short-lived. I am convinced only if they lead to action. The guards in Auschwitz listened to Mozart at night and turned on the gas in the morning. Can art like yours save us from our hearts of stone?

S: For me the exposure to suffering, even in the unreality of the theatre, is meant to induce a conversion towards compassion. In one of my early comedies I surprised people with a sober ending, and one that has puzzled many commentators. In *Love's Labour's Lost* I showed a group of men and women playing sophisticated games with one another and hiding their real feelings behind a façade of words. Then in the very last scene comes the shock of death, and this leads to a decision to do penance. The lovers are sent for a year to serve the dying in hospital before they can be sure that their love is genuine. The leading joker, Berowne, 'a man replete with mocks', is told to

> Visit the speechless sick, and still converse
> With groaning wretches; and your task shall be,
> With all the fierce endeavour of your wit
> To enforce the pained impotent to smile.

This ending, I hoped, could jolt the audience into seriousness about mortality.

R: Certainly hearts learn from being present to pain, but can a fiction change people really?

S: In each of my tragedies I arrived at depths of horror about Act III but in later acts there was a different feeling. A movement towards peace, costly peace. Ideally the audience shares that process.

R: When I had the courage to be present to oppressed people, at first it shook me. But the shock gave way to a sense of admiration and of hope. Contact with them changed me. I began to see life through the eyes of others and understood, as never before, that love has to take sides in this world of violence.

S: You sound like my King Lear! He started as a proud and angry old man. Then everything collapsed around him. He found himself reduced to poverty, wandering alone in a storm, even afraid that he was losing his mind. At one point he meets a naked beggar called Poor Tom. In contact with a world he had never encountered before, he realises that he had always avoided his people's pain. In a gesture that would have been incredible to the previous Lear, he invites the beggar to go ahead of him into the shelter. And then he cries out with his new vision:

> Poor naked wretches, wheresoe'er you are,
> That bide the pelting of this pitiless night,
> How shall our houseless heads and unfed sides,
> Your looped and windowed raggedness, defend you
> From seasons such as these? O, I have ta'en
> Too little care of this! Take physic, pomp;
> Expose thyself to feel what wretches feel,
> That thou mayst shake the superflux to them
> And show the heavens more just.

R: You have the basis of liberation theology there! The conversion starts from a real encounter with poverty – and not from watching it on television. Your speech even captures the desire for solidarity with victims, as we say today, and the suggestion that we reveal a different God through a different sharing of the world's goods. Like Lear, I had been shielded from that struggling side of life. And I was changed through meeting the poor face to face.

S: It is a strange avenue of wisdom. People do not usually think of the pain of others as a source of liberation. Even from watching a tragedy like *King Lear* an audience finds that feelings are deepened. They join the heart-journey of the king himself. They move from safe horizons into turmoil and then into sympathy.

From revenge towards forgiveness

R: There is a Christian paradox in all this. Out of evil and darkness God can bring goodness and light. It is the journey of Good Friday to Easter Sunday.

S: I was a Christian of course but, at least for my imagination, religion often lacked the guts to delve into the darkness. It failed to do justice to the pain always there behind the bright scenery of life.

R: If religion becomes too cosy, it cannot feel the hurts of history. Don't most human tragedies remain undramatic? A Hamlet or a King Lear enter into intense situations of agony or failure. But in ordinary lives the panic is numb, daily, and hidden. That is true of the majority of the world's poor. And the poor have always been the majority.

S: We artists tend to specialise in intensity, but to give reality to those ordinary burdens.

R: Is it one of the dangers of literature to remain too personal? Our situation is not just individual tragedy multiplied but a whole system gone sick. Initially I thought of my ministry as helping people, full stop. When I discovered that the struggles around me were bigger than the personal, it altered my way of praying the gospels. I saw that Jesus was murdered by a religious system that could not tolerate his vision. I realised that the tragedies of history have to do with power and its temptations.

S: Perhaps I never connected the evils of the powerful with the pain of the poor as you do, but in my later years I moved towards a Christian theme – forgiveness of old hurts and resentments.

R: If we have been victimised, it seems hard not to nourish resentment. To forgive those who persecute us is pure grace. It is the most radical of Christian calls.

S: It was the struggle of my last hero, Prospero. In *The Tempest* he is put in a position of power over his old enemies. I show him full of dangerous and unreconciled feelings, until a key moment when he learns that without forgiveness there is no wisdom. He learns this from the spirit-figure Ariel, who surprises him by saying 'your affections would become tender' if Prospero could see the suffering of his enemies. And Prospero comes to the insight that 'the rarer action is in virtue than in vengeance'.

R: Often at the end of a tiring day I visited one of the small communities of the poor and found even my physical strength renewed. The injustice angered me. But harder to cope with personally was the opposition of some of my fellow bishops. I could take their disagreement but behind-my-back manoeuvres left me confused and bitter at times. Forgiveness was always an uphill battle for me – humanly it seemed impossible. Is it significant that it came to you towards the end of your life?

S: My imagination led me beyond tragedy towards this healing of attitudes. It seemed a further layer of the spiritual adventure. Before the end of life you want to let go of bitterness and gather everything together in peace.

R: From different worlds I think we agree on basics. If I am too shielded from the world's pain, I am in danger of sleepwalking through life. Taking the risk of really being present to suffering will first disturb us, leave us helpless, and can open doors to compassion. Beyond that again, there is an unexpected mountain of forgiveness to climb.

A costly wisdom

S: We both trusted passionate incarnation rather than theory. We wanted to make the cost of the human journey real to people. We hoped to remind them of the full range of their humanity.

R: Being present to the wounded ones of the world breaks down our prisons of pettiness. I felt impotent before such brutality, and yet reaching my limits was good for me. The powerlessness pushed me to trust beyond myself, ultimately to trust in God.

S: I wanted my audience to be taken beyond themselves by what they saw, to recognise their own hidden pain, and in this way to be – as you might say – converted. Our own vulnerability is mirrored back to us through the brokenness of others.

R: That is what God is always doing in our reluctant humanity, transforming 'hearts of stone into hearts of flesh'. As an artist you did something similar.

S: It meant descending into the darker regions of humanity before being able to imagine roads towards harmony.

R: You are echoing there the journey of Christ himself.

S: His journey was first of all an experience. I see the gospels as drama, not just because I am a dramatist.

R: Christ's journey is still an experience and a drama – made real in the pain of ordinary people and in the slow erosion of our egoism. History is not the neutral place I thought it to be: it is a battleground between love and hate. Taking sides in this struggle brought me into more joy and more agony than I had ever imagined. I came alive as never before, and eventually it cost me my life.

S: Hamlet and Lear and even Othello entered into an aliveness beyond agony. There was a costly wisdom beyond the darkness. But it has to be embodied. I did it in drama. You did it in the drama of your witness.

R: So we both followed our call – to taste the cup of life to the full, which meant entering areas of agony and even cruelty. When times were toughest for me, my prayer became a simple plea, to be worthy of the suffering of the poor.

S: And I came to trust that there was another quality of mercy and peace beyond all the pain, and one that pointed towards a religious horizon. In the mouth of Hamlet facing death, 'There's a special providence in the fall of a sparrow . . . the readiness is all'.

REFLECTION SPACE

In a lecture of 1976 the theologian Bernard Lonergan evokes the blindness to social suffering that afflicts our humanity and comments in words that could be put into the mouth of Oscar Romero:

> To my mind the only solution is religious. What will sweep away the rationalizations? . . . when reasoning is ineffective, what is left but faith? What will smash the determinisms – economic, social, cultural, psychological – that egotism has

constructed and exploited? What can be offered but the hoping beyond hope that religion inspires? . . . what is needed is not retributive justice but self-sacrificing love.

Two poets in different ways evoke the nocturnal imagination of the world's hidden pain:

> I wake and feel the fell of dark, not day.
> What hours, O what black hours we have spent
> This night, what sights you, heart, saw; ways you went!
> (Gerard Manley Hopkins)

> The fox eats its own leg in the trap
> To go free. As it limps through the grass
> The earth itself appears to bleed.
> When the morning light comes up
> Who knows what suffering midnight was?
> Proof is what I do not need.
> (from 'Proof' by Brendan Kennelly)

A third poet, Elizabeth Jennings, crosses the threshold into awe at how some can face and transform the suffering of those around them. Her 'Night Sister' tells of a nurse in a psychiatric hospital who radiates 'compassion' in a 'world of fears'.

> How is it possible not to grow hard
> To build a shell around yourself when you
> Have to watch so much pain?
> . . . we cannot dare to show
> Our sickness. But you listen and we know
> That you can meet us in our own distress.

CHAPTER 5

SOLITUDE AND SILENCE

People are in every way prevented from getting inside themselves. Our greatest problem is a fear of depth.

(Thomas Merton)

Solitude is essentially the discovery and acceptance of our uniqueness.

(Lawrence Freeman)

Pascal remarked that all humanity's problems arise from people who are incapable of sitting alone in their own room. Jean Baudrillard describes post-modern culture as one that 'has lost the formula for stopping'. What is the tone of being-with-myself? Is it a shallow, almost embarrassed encounter? Or can it be a zone of presence and listening, where another kind of wisdom is learned? More hidden than friendship or failure or the impact of tragedy is the whole area of being alone and of the quality of one's self-quiet.

I have met many people in times of struggle and I have tried not to influence their deciding but rather to be, as Socrates might say, a midwife to their disposition of freedom. This means fostering a space of self-listening that people often lack. Although this midwifery is never a mere technique, it seems to involve two stages of growth. The first comes from being taken seriously and being appreciated in one's honesty. I am surprised at how rare this can be in people's lives. Many suffer from fragmentation and may seldom have the opportunity to hear their real selves. If this first stage involves a shift of wavelength – through being heard and trusted – a second stage allows the person to realise that he or she has a powerful zone of quiet within. Although someone else can help you to find the doorway, you can only enter this zone on your own.

Solitude is not the same as loneliness. It is a self-chosen space, rooted in a recognition that nobody else can live my life. Similarly silence is not the absence of noise: it is a quality of presence and of attention. The experience of solitude and silence is like music that can be played in two different keys. There is the initial major key, so to speak, of the courage to be alone and to listen deeply. It is normal to enjoy a certain consolation here: it is the fruit of a life that is flowing generously. But there is a second key, a minor key, when solitude and silence take on frightening tones.

HOLY SATURDAY DESCENT

One of the unique features of the theology of Hans Urs von Balthasar was his retrieval of the Holy Saturday experience. Christ's going down into 'hell' was usually interpreted as a moment of victory and liberation. There are famous icons showing him standing on the cross and raising Adam and Eve by the hand. Balthasar saw the strange silence of Holy Saturday as a moment of total abandonment and despair, a lonely and numb descent into the realm of the dead. Instead of being a preview of the victory of Easter, it symbolises the bottom of an abyss, a going down 'into the last futility of empty time and hopeless death'. It goes beyond even the terrible scene of Calvary. It enters a realm dominated by death.

In this spirit Holy Saturday becomes the moment where life has no meaning, where the void is dominant, and where people feel crushed and beyond the reach of any hope. When such desolation strikes, no light reaches into that dungeon and – as in the Book of Job – cheap words are insulting. It is tempting to speak of silence and solitude as if they were always comfortable, strengthening and peace-giving. It seems attractive to escape from the noisy self and to reach an inner oasis of the Spirit. However, there is another silence-solitude that is more crucifying than consoling. It is marked by impotence, a lostness beyond words, a complete numbness of hope. I have glimpsed it in those suffering from terminal illness (at least when the news first comes). I have witnessed it with friends in the world of addiction, when everything is hurting, body and heart and soul. Or in those who suffer from mental illness, when all is chaos and confusion and nobody seems to understand. Or indeed in ordinary people who can experience a brush with nothingness in many forms.

DISTURBING SPACES OF SILENCE

Before all greatness, be silent – in art, in music, in religion: silence.

(Friedrich von Hügel)

Several great novels of the twentieth century evoke spaces of disturbing mystery. For instance, both E. M. Forster in *A Passage to India* (1924) and Patrick White in *Voss* (1957) bring their characters to languages beyond ordinary words. And they both satirise the poverty of conventional religious language as incapable of nourishing the deeper ranges of spiritual experience.

Mrs Moore is the embodiment of religious awareness in *A Passage to India*, who finds that her visit to India expands her sense of mystery in ways both liberating and frightening. In a conversation with her administrator son Ronny, she happens to

mention 'God', only to realise at once that it was a mistake to say
that word. He 'approved of religion as long as it endorsed the
National Anthem, but objected when it attempted to influence
his life'. As Mrs Moore aged, God was more constantly in her
thoughts,

> though oddly enough he satisfied her less. She needs must
> pronounce his name frequently, as the greatest she knew,
> yet she had never found it less efficacious. Outside the arch
> there seemed always an arch, beyond the remotest echo a
> silence.

At a more negative stage of her journey, Mrs Moore thinks of
'poor little talkative Christianity', with all its 'divine words' as
simply an echo chamber of emptiness. Mrs Moore's experience
captures the tension present in any contemplative adventure in
silence. You go beyond usual words and usual knowing, into a
'cloud of unknowing', where ordinary words can seem tired and
fruitless. Anyone who has the courage to visit this inner 'India'
will find themselves drawn through 'arches' and beyond common sense. To quote a more recent novel (Saul Bellow's *Herzog*),
'Go through what is comprehensible and you conclude that only
the incomprehensible gives any light'.

The Australian novelist Patrick White was quite open
about his desire to 'convey a splendour, a transcendence, which
is there, above human realities'. In one of his later works he
wrote:

> 'Love' is an exhausted word, and God has been expelled by
> those who know better, but I offer you the one as proof that
> the other still exists.

In this spirit his epic novel *Voss* explores how people arrive at
love and at a sense of God through risking silence and solitude.
To take one key insight in the novel: when feverish with illness
Laura, the lover of Voss, voices her vision to her incomprehend-
ing and embarrassed doctor: 'When man is truly humbled,
when he has learnt that he is not God, then he is nearest to

becoming so.' Much later, as an old lady, she is being asked about her life, and her relationship with the famous explorer. 'Knowledge was never a matter of geography. Quite the reverse, it overflows all maps that exist.'

In their different ways both Forster and White want to rescue their readers from prisons of practicality and confront them with deeper wavelengths of the spirit. Their characters undergo something of the inner ordeal that we will glimpse later through the figures of Thérèse and Nietzsche.

ALONENESS OF DEATH

Tolstoy's *The Death of Ivan Illich* is a powerful evocation of the fruits of lonely vulnerability as against the burdens of playing a false role. Ivan knows he is dying even though everyone around him – from his wife to the doctors – pretend that a cure is being found. This man of social prestige, still in his mid-forties, had paid a heavy price for his success. His marriage has been unhappy in spite of all his wealth. He now finds himself utterly alone in his pain, and weeps from his isolation and his sense of there being no God. Into this bleak landscape of uncontrollable pain comes a young man called Gerasim, a strong peasant who is to act as a servant on night duty for him. In fact he becomes much more. Gerasim has no difficulty in assisting Ivan in the most embarrassing duties such as going to the toilet. Nor does he avoid the fact of death: 'we will all die, so why should I object to helping out.' The symbol of this new relationship is in the fact – shocking to Ivan's wife – that Ivan finds it easy to sleep if Gerasim supports his feet on his shoulders for hours on end. This is a story of arriving at the core of human needs, even in the aloneness of death. Ivan sees through the sham of his life, its priorities and choices, but he discovers extraordinary serenity in allowing himself to be weak and dependent, and in accepting the silent tenderness of Gerasim.

He used to send for Gerasim so that he could rest his feet on those shoulders and have a chat with him. The servant did all this willingly, with a simplicity, a goodness, a naturalness that touched Ivan deeply. With all other members of his family circle, their aliveness and their very health seemed an affront to the dying man, but the youthfulness and strength of Gerasim consoled him and left him in peace. What caused him the greatest pain was the falsity all around, the lie adopted by everyone that he was only sick but not dying, that all he needed was to get some treatment and rest and then everything would work out well.

The presence of Gerasim allows Ivan to descend into the depths of his solitude and to accept that he is really dying. Although he experiences moments of sheer hate for his wife and family, he suppresses any hurtful expressions of this. When at the end he undergoes three days of intense pain, he manages to arrive at a moment of compassion for his family. He sees the panic of his teenage son and tears on the face of his wife. 'I am causing them to suffer. It is better for them if I go.' In a final moment he summons up energy to point to his son and say to his wife, 'Take him away, have pity on him.' Then comes a moment where Ivan wants to say 'forgive' and says instead 'let go'. (The two terms sound similar in Russian.) It is almost his last word. The pain seems to disappear. The fear is no more. He experiences a great light. 'So this is it,' he cried aloud. 'What joy!' He hears someone say 'It is all over' and within himself he thinks, 'death does not exist any more'.

The rhythm of this little masterpiece leads the reader through pain of many kinds towards a threshold of light and of forgiveness. Indeed Tolstoy's story could have fitted equally in our chapters on vulnerability or on tragedy, rather than here on solitude. Many creative artists, such as Francis Bacon, offer disturbing visions of our reluctance to face this shadow side of each life, but some also hint at costly journeys towards surprising light.

CONTRASTING
CONTEMPORARIES

Loneliness does not torture: it matures.

(Nietzsche)

If others were to realise the trials I am undergoing, what a surprise it would be.

(Thérèse of Lisieux)

The dialogue of this chapter brings together two prophetic figures, who in totally different ways entered agonised zones of silence and solitude. Saint Thérèse of Lisieux and Friedrich Nietzsche are unlikely interlocutors. In history they had never heard of one another. But they were contemporaries, and in a strange sense companion spirits. Nietzsche was born nearly thirty years earlier than Thérèse, and as a philosopher became the symbol of a radical rejection of God – but in a spirit of alarm rather than of triumph. When, in January 1889, he embraced a horse that was being whipped in Turin and then entered a mental illness that never left him until his death in 1900, Thérèse was in her first year as a Carmelite novice. Seven years later came the chapter in her life that makes her a possible dialogue partner for Nietzsche – her dramatic eighteen months of crisis of faith.

Largely because of this final phase in the young saint's life, Thérèse and Nietzsche have been brought together by other authors. In 1984 Noelle Hausman wrote a book in French comparing their horizons. In 2000 a Carmelite Sister, Bridget Edman, won an international religious drama competition for a play entitled *Roses have Thorns*, which offered various lyrical interactions between Thérèse and Friedrich. Sister Bridget is of Swedish Lutheran origin and lives in a convent in South Africa. The imagined dialogue that I offer here is different and yet partly inspired by these two writers.

Both Nietzsche and Thérèse grew up in intensely religious

families. Nietzsche's father and grandfather were Lutheran ministers. Thérèse's father had wanted to become a priest but opted instead for exceptional religious commitment as a married man. Three of her sisters had entered the same Carmelite convent when Thérèse, as the baby of the family, entered with special permission at the age of 15. Although she and Nietzsche took diametrically different directions in life, they both share a radical desire to go the whole way. As a result they were misunderstood by most of those around them, and it was only after their deaths that their genius became known through what they had written; in both cases their writings were initially published (with some censorship) by their respective sisters.

Nietzsche is often wrongly portrayed as a proud godfather of modern atheism. In fact his celebrated claim that 'God is dead' was put into the mouth of a madman, mocked by his hearers in the marketplace, and was less a cry of victory than a recognition of a loss to be mourned: 'How could we drink up the ocean? Who gave us a sponge to wipe away the whole horizon?' Ancient meanings had become incredible. Nietzsche sensed himself first as a prophet of monumental murder and only later as a searcher for a new artistic 'yes' with which to live. The old idea of God had functioned not just as an illusion but as 'a crime against life'. For him 'love is the state in which we see things as they are *not*'.

In this spirit, Nietzsche often voiced hatred for Christianity, viewing it as a life-denying and pessimistic oppression of humanity, but he retained a strange admiration for the person of Jesus. He represented 'the best example of an ideal life' which 'in my heart I have never rejected'. Jesus was a 'holy anarchist', an 'unbeliever' in all forms of 'spiritual pride and puritanism'. As he once remarked, 'When I wage war against Christianity, the most serious Christians have always been well-disposed to me'.

Even a few selected quotations (from *The Anti-Christ*) can give the flavour of Nietzsche's unusually positive sense of Jesus:

There was only one Christian and he died on the cross.

He suffers, he loves, *with* those, *in* those who are doing evil to him.

It is not a 'belief' which is the mark of a Christian: the Christian is distinguished by a different way of acting.

It is not penance nor prayer for forgiveness that leads to God; only living according to the gospel leads to God, it *is* God.

Faith *lives*, it resists formulas.

His eloquent description of Dionysius (in *Beyond Good and Evil*) seems to echo his admiration for Jesus:

The genius of the heart silences all that is loud and self-satisfied, teaching it to listen; he smooths rough souls and lets them taste a new desire, to remain as still as a mirror . . .

From his touch everyone walks away enriched within, newer to oneself than before, broken open, more unsure, more tender, more fragile, more vulnerable, and full of hopes that as yet have no name.

And here, from *Thus Spake Zarathustra*, is part of Nietzsche's remarkable hymn of human hopes – words that could serve as a bridge of sympathy towards someone like Thérèse:

I love those whose souls are deep, even in being
    wounded.
I love those whose souls are overflowing so that they
    forget themselves.
I love those who have free spirits and free hearts.

It is clearly false to Nietzsche to portray him as a closed and bitter atheist. If the true picture of him is closer to prophetic critique of religion than is often thought, the real Thérèse is very far from the image of her as the 'Little Flower', simply the advocate of an attractive 'little way' of childlike trust and innocence. As other writings of hers emerged in the decades after her death, her story changed. She is now known to have experienced a painful eclipse of faith in her last two years. And it was during this time of trial (her favourite word in her diary was 'épreuve') that she felt called, as she put it, to sit at the table of non-believers and to share their 'bread of pain'.

Up to this point in her young life – she was only 23 when this crisis came – her religious life had been suffused with joy and simplicity. Her entry into 'this dark tunnel' was provoked by an insight about unbelievers. Previously she had pondered the question of people who declared themselves atheists, but she had never believed in the reality of their unbelief. Their words surely did not represent a serious choice, she felt. But now 'Jesus made me feel that there are really souls without faith'. Her insight into the lived actuality of atheism leads her immediately to see unbelievers as her 'brothers', to an identification with them in a void of feeling which she embraces in a missionary spirit on their behalf. Thus she enters her long months of 'temptations against faith'.

In her diary she notes that a fairy tale chapter of her life had ended. Ever since childhood, she says, she had longed for heaven by contrast with the sadness of earth (a stance that Nietzsche would surely pounce upon with derision). Now she describes inner voices that mock her old serenity: 'You dream of light, of a country of sweet perfumes . . . you think you will one day leave behind the surrounding fog . . . Go ahead, rejoice in a death that will give you . . . only a darker night, the night of nothingness ('la nuit du néant').' And when she wrote those last words in French she added ' . . .' as if to indicate inexpressible depths of despair.

One of the conversions of Nietzsche's life came in a solitary experience in the mountains in 1881 when he found 'new vision' through being 'enraptured and taken out of' himself. From then on he sensed a quasi-redemptive vocation as a celebrant of humanity. But this would mean, he saw, 'leading one of the most dangerous of lives', even measuring himself secretly against Jesus. During the last decade of his sanity he identified himself increasingly as an explorer of unknown territories in human imagination, but eventually it led him across the brink into permanent breakdown. Thérèse, by contrast, records no mystical experiences but finds herself called beyond the ordinary pieties of her religious culture and towards a dangerous mission in the land of nihilists. Intellectually she had practically no awareness of the crises of her age but intuitively she entered into depths of struggle just as much as Nietzsche.

Nietzsche was so accurate in his fiery anger against complacent religion and grey thinking: we are made for more exciting realms than are dreamt of in average religion. But his hatred of smallness is where Nietzsche goes sour. He becomes a believer in power alone and incapable of any tone of trust or – a word he would despise – love. Thérèse is his equal in ambition for fullness of life, but her secret lies in a trust of smallness, a source of strength beyond what he could imagine, and which was her anchor even in her darkest moment of eclipsed faith. Both of them explored depths that exist in all of us but which few have the courage to face or the language to express.

DIALOGUE INTO DARKNESS

It is night – I live in my own light. I drink the flames from my own inner fire.

(Nietzsche, in Bridget Edman's *Roses have Thorns*)

I cannot think of life without the darkness now. The darkness is God's gift to me. Yet I am afraid.

(Thérèse, in *Roses have Thorns*)

As in some other conversations in this book, almost exact quotations from Nietzsche and Thérèse will be marked by italics in this text. The dialogue takes many liberties and goes beyond anything we know of their explicit statements.

Clash of yes and no

N: You are exactly the kind of person I despise – a weak woman, cringing before a God in the hope of eternity, suppressing your human instincts, locking yourself up in this symbol of unreality, and pretending to do everything because of love.

T: My way of life can be cowardly, if it does not dare to go the whole way. I would love you to know me not just from the outside. I am no longer a silly child in search of comfort.

N: Just a sick young woman with illusions of sanctity, *false to the point of innocence.*

T: I'm not afraid of your contempt. At least not for myself. Perhaps I am afraid of it for you. What does it do to you, this constantly destructive passion of yours?

N: I am not destructive. My passion is to live a huge yes. But there is so much rubbish in the way. I hate cramped and small lives. My vocation is to disturb them.

T: I too have a mission. My small life wants to be a huge yes. And certainly, there is rubbish around, even in the spiritual piety of my convent.

N: A temple to an escapist 'no' to life.

T: Even you have to say a small 'no' – to make space for your bigger 'yes'. My mission is to awaken the world to the call of love.

N: And how will they hear the alarm clock? Are you writing explosive pages like I am?

T: Perhaps yes. I am writing about myself and about the littleness and the darkness of love, even the terrible darkness of God. You have not seen my pages any more than I have seen yours.

N: Perhaps you have visited some minor darkness. But you have chosen to cling to a grim trust in God. That's where we differ. I choose perilous strength. You choose infantile weakness. You sacrifice everything for the 'salvation of your soul', mere spiritual egoism, making *the world revolve around you.* You are afraid to live.

T: I am not afraid to love. And to me to love is to live. My deepest fear is not to love – to waste this life, making everything revolve around me.

N: I too have a horror of waste and of not embracing the risk of depth. But that involves a rare and disturbing road.

T: Of course it does. All my life since the age of twelve, I have asked to be disturbed every day into greater space for love.

N: Who is there to ask? 'God', I suppose. I have only my own will to live from. We have to invent our lives ourselves.

T: You sound too lonely in those depths. Is there no relationship? Is there only your power of will and your suspicion of all the old answers?

N: I deliberately cultivate a mixture of power and suspicion. To protect that road you need to be lonely – so as not to become one of the herd.

Risking the darkness

T: I know the sense of utter loneliness but it is never the total truth. Embracing the darkness in solitude is a form of love.

N: Love is just a word for a feeling we like to have. It masks our lust for self-comfort.

T: No, it is a flow that starts from another Person. I know, even in darkness, *the presence of a Face.*

N: For a moment I thought we had more in common. Now I hear the boring old fairy-tale about a friendly God secretly beside us. A fantasy children need to see them through the night! The source of mediocrity in adults who can't face reality!

T: But what if children were right? They trust naturally. You cannot trust, it seems.

N: I once wrote that the *child is the climax of wisdom. We are not to be camels, carrying every burden, or lions, roaring in anger. But children who have the innocence to cry a Yes to life.*

T: I know your camels and your lions too. There are so many burdens and so much to resent. The child does not banish the camel and the lion but embraces them.

N: That sounds too girlish, too *unmanly*. Can you embrace the insane dark?

T: When I can't see my lover and can't feel him, trusting becomes an agony, an absence, an emptiness. I am terrified by my own thoughts when that darkness lasts. I am plagued by doubts at least in the mind.

N: Only in the mind?

T: My heart tries to stay steady in spite of my imagination. I hear inner voices that mock me. They tell me that all is illusion, that there is no God, no heaven, that I am wasting my little life in this impossible fantasy of loving. Perhaps there is nobody to love. That is the most terrible thought.

N: I was about to join the mocking voices. I was about to attack your flight from reality. It seemed too serene to be real. But you got there ahead of me. We are twins in at least one thing: you also know something of agony and dark aloneness.

T: My worry is that you have embraced agony as an idol. Your anger about the smallness of God leaves your imagination with no space for a larger God. You seem an honest but terribly divided man.

N: And you are an honest but terribly innocent girl. Yours is a world I have left behind. I saw into a cultural earthquake that makes all those securities impossible. Yes, I am a divided man. That is my fate, which I live sometimes as tragedy and sometimes as joy.

T: Your atheism seems a kind of 'piety'. If you really followed the passion in you, faith need not mean going back to the damaged God but being found by the liberating One.

N: Too soft for me, my dear. I have seen through the snares of false desire. I have seen through the misuse of power in the name of religion. It is too sick to be believed by someone who has passed through my crucible of suspicion. I can only believe in my own urge to create. The religious urge, set free from the old forms of 'god', can give birth to great art.

T: What you call the old forms of God are what killed Jesus.

N: Do not talk to me of him. His beauty haunts me in spite of my hatred of his followers.

T: His beauty was to go into the darkness out of love. And we both, with all our differences, try to echo his courage. We both know that the dark is terrible but the only way. You have dared to enter areas most people don't even imagine. Out of the depths you have cried, I am sure, in your writings.

N: Nobody has ever dared recognise me in those depths. Can a little nun like you grasp my agony and my aloneness?

T: I choose to share them. I have lost all feeling of faith. I have crossed lonely thresholds where nobody understands. *Love alone survives.*

N: Every great human explorer is *more afraid of being understood than of being misunderstood.* I will go mad because I cannot believe in love.

T: You might go mad if you cannot receive in love. Darkness without trust is a danger zone.

N: There is no protection, no trust.

T: I will be both for you, if you let me.

N: You are amazing but I fear incredible.

T: I am incredible because you see no power in littleness, in surrender, in a child's confidence. That is my secret which allows me to dare the dark.

N: And my fate is that I confront depths and darks naked, without shields, utterly alone, like a man. I have never surrendered.

T: You are too alone my friend. Terribly so.

Moments of breakthrough

N: To me you still represent all that I despise in Christianity – its *ascetical ideal, its disgust with life, its slave mentality, its hatred of the senses,* its escape into eternity. *Religion is sickness, born out of fear and need.* Do you not see that you killed your humanity when you entered the convent?

T: I know the dangers you are talking about. They were real for me in earlier years. My family, like yours, was 'ascetical' in its faith. It seemed right to flee from life, thinking that I was seeking God. But experiences have made me move on. I left behind that older language when I found myself invited into frightening depths. I needed to be pruned of my safer pieties.

N: What kind of turning points could you have found, remaining within this terrible structure of your nunnery?

T: I had several turning points but perhaps two main ones. The first was before I entered Carmel. It happened at Christmas, a week before my fourteenth birthday. A small episode provoked a major change. I overheard my father comment that it was just as well this was the last time for the childhood custom of Christmas stockings. My first reaction was typical of me: I nearly burst into tears. But then I crossed a threshold in myself. I went downstairs as an adult, playing the old tradition with a new lightness. My father was delighted. In that *night of light, I rediscovered a strength of spirit that I had lost at four and a half* when my mother died. I had taken my life into my own hands. I became strong. I stopped being a sensitive victim.

N: To my surprise I like what you say. The adult child, who emerges from childishness into power – to live a difficult 'yes'. And the second turning point?

T: I mentioned it already. It is what most brings us together. It also happened at a feast, at Easter ten years later. I had lived with eyes on eternity and those eyes went blind. And that blindness forced me to embrace a darker companionship, dare I say, with you and people like you who cannot believe the old story in the old way. Of course I struggled against the terrible thoughts but they continued to plague me. I heard voices making fun of all my hopes: '*Go ahead, rejoice in a death that will give you . . . only a darker night, the night of nothingness*'.

N: But it was only a pious game for you. You were playing with danger but safe in the 'hands of God'.

Companions on the edge

T: You of all people should understand me: I was both in danger and desperate in my trusting. It was not a game. It was an agony. I once imagined suicide. I held on to hope with no help from my feelings. It was like a madness I had to hide from others, but which gave me a whole new mission.

N: Yes, I should understand you. You echo my many moments of living out on the edge, even though my depth journeys were so different.

T: Tell me something of your turning points.

N: I had so many. But there was one revelation that I never could fully express, because it shook all my previous foundations. Like yours it happened at a definite time and place, in my beloved mountains at Sils Maria in August 1881. I sensed myself caught up into an eternal becoming, an *eternal return*, and knew myself fated to proclaim *a sacred Yes to all of humanity*. It was mysticism without God, except that I was put, terribly, in the place of God. *That was the moment in which I brought to birth* my new vision and only *my love for that moment* allowed me to endure the isolation of all these years.

T: Why are you sure it was 'without God'?

N: Because for me the only God I knew was impossible, a tyrant, a power, an insult.

T: And yet you speak so tenderly of Jesus.

N: I could never connect those two words together: Jesus and God.

T: Unless they meet, neither word makes sense. Jesus transformed God! He tore away those masks of tyranny that made you suffer for so long.

N: I cannot, simply cannot, trust that simplicity.

T: Because you cling to your shield of suspicion. Would you hope to destroy my faith?

N: Not any more. I thought it was the usual weak and demeaning thing but it is not. It is real for you, deep and costly. Such *genuine faith does not deceive. It fulfils whatever the believer expects*. You have come from poverty into power.

T: But not on my own, only with Jesus.

N: There we part company, as you know.

T: Not completely, because I want to share your road too.

N: Earlier I would have spat at that remark as condescending. Now I do not reject you. When we are gone people will discover us through our words.

T: Yes, I feel many will read my words.

N: What will they find?

T: That childhood is wisdom. That God is tenderness rather than power, and yet rupture rather than repose. That daily life is the place of our love adventure. That there is light at first and then terrible darkness. That our solitude and our silence are spaces of encounter, sources of flourishing. That beneath all the suspicion lies an ocean of trust without shadows.

N: Your confidence rings foreign to me, but in our different light and our different dark, you are a strange companion.

T: So we can be com-panions, *sharing the same bread.*

N: *You believe. I seek.* But, I now see, you also seek – like a real saint, like a real artist.

T: I also want to be a priest and poet of yes – like you!

N: You are different. You are like – a divine comedy.

REFLECTION SPACE

Drawing again on Sebastian Moore: Only in silent solitude comes 'the most revealing experience that we have: a sense that I am *in myself* and not relatively to other people and to my culture'. If I stay with that 'in myself' experience, I discover not just desire-as-need but, more surprisingly, a sense of being significant because I am desired by God.

Borrowing from Jean Vanier: Seven dimensions of love are necessary for 'the transformation of the heart of those who are profoundly lonely'. They are: to reveal their value, to understand, to communicate, to celebrate, to empower, to be in communion with another, and, finally, to forgive.

Solitude is one of the most precious things in the human spirit. It is different from loneliness. When you are lonely, you become acutely conscious of your own separation. Solitude can be a homecoming to your own deepest belonging.

(John O'Donoghue)

Silence and solitude can be healing. They can also be searing. There is a world of difference between Wordsworth's evening 'quiet as a nun, breathless with adoration' and Hopkins'

O the mind, mind has mountains, cliffs of fall
Frightful, sheer, no-man-fathomed. Hold them cheap
May who ne'er hung there.

And from another poet, Ernesto Cardenal:

We want God's voice to be clear but it is not. It is deep as night, with a dark clarity like an x-ray. It reaches our bones.

CHAPTER 6

RIVER OF THE ORDINARY

There lives the dearest freshness deep down things.
(Gerard Manley Hopkins)

Transforming moments of life come through friendships, even through failures, through the cries of others, or through the strangeness of silence. In each of these zones we found that there were thresholds to cross. And the courage to cross them is where our human adventure can open towards God. But there is another human space where we spend much of our lives — in the valleys of daily non-intensity. What about the ordinary days, where chores accumulate and tired attitudes can take over? And yet within everyday dullness lies a different threshold to be crossed. Here also slow wisdom is possible and a quieter poetry can point towards Mystery.

A PARABLE OF DOLPHINS

One of Ireland's leading scholars of Celtic spirituality and folk-lore spoke on the radio as I was writing these pages. John Moriarty (author of *Turtle was gone a long time*) offered listeners a parable-tale found in various cultures. It tells of a collector of shellfish who found himself marooned for the night on a rock when the tide came in. To this rock dolphins came in the darkness and, shedding their skins, revealed themselves as beautiful human beings. Before dawn they all returned to the sea, but the man had taken one of the skins, leaving one of the women without her dolphin-self. She follows him home across the sand and marries him. All goes normally until one day, when she is making bread, a drop of dolphin oil falls from the ceiling on to the kitchen table. The smell brings her back to another sense of herself. She searches and finds the skin hidden in the roof, puts it on and returns to the ocean.

John Moriarty meditated on how hints of the eternal show themselves in the midst of ordinary life. We live immersed in the small demands of each day. But that is not the whole story. What is our true identity? We are more than we seem. From time to time we experience 'intimations of immortality'. How can we be faithful to the two worlds that we are, the obvious world and the more mysterious one? Where are the dolphin drops that recall us to what is eternal in us?

REDISCOVERING THE CELTIC

The label 'Celtic' has become fashionable in recent times and unites strange bedfellows. In Dublin there is a 'Celtic Healing Centre' that offers acupuncture and yoga sessions. The last time I checked, I found 2319 Internet sites dealing with Celtic Spirituality. Even if ambiguous fads masquerade under this heading, as a cultural explosion it remains significant. It meets some of the hungers of this 'post-modern' moment. It expresses a perennial quest of the imagination, one that was neglected during the long reign of efficiency called 'modernity'.

What is so attractive about the popular image of 'Celtic'? Why does it seem to answer some re-emerging needs of the spirit? Perhaps because the Celtic sensibility viewed ordinary life as a place of divine presence. It discerned minor miracles in everyday things, from eating to the changes of the weather. It viewed creation and the events of life as shot through with mystery. It

reverenced sacred places of healing. In this way Celtic spirituality offers a down-to-earth immanence, where God together with
saints and angels protect people from danger and accompany
them in their chores, burdens, fears and joys. The visible and the
invisible interact. The eternal and the everyday converge.

A 'post-modern' sensibility, in its more positive tones,
searches out such convergences to overcome our sense of frag-
mented living. We want roots to save us from an invasion of
surface images. We are more open about the divine (even if
hesitant about the definiteness of the God of Jesus Christ). No
doubt we reread the Celtic story selectively, and not always with
historical accuracy. But this whole phenomenon is evidence of
a desire to find larger spaces for our everyday selves. 'Only connect', wrote E. M. Forster as the epigraph of his novel *Howards
End*. The Celtic imagination seems to suggest ways of
rediscovering wholeness within the ordinary.

MAGIC REALISM
IRISH-STYLE

One of the most enchanting (and successful) novels to emerge
from Ireland in recent years is *Four Letters of Love* by Niall
Williams (published in 1997). It reads like a lyrical hymn not
only to human love but to healing presences at work in people's
lives. If Latin American writers are labelled as 'magic realists'
when they go beyond the limits of common sense, Niall
Williams has created a Celtic version of the same school. The
very poetry of his style shows 'the hopeless inadequacy of the
human mind to fathom the miracle of love'.

Few Latin American novels, however, are so unshy of the
word 'God' (even though Williams is not writing 'religious fiction' in the conventional sense). Twice in the last page we are
told that 'the plots of love and God are one and the same thing'.
We are given a flowing celebration of the love between Nicholas
and Isabel, a love capable of overcoming tragedy, as shown in

the restoration to life and music of Isabel's handicapped brother Sean.

Two philosophies clash throughout these pages. There is a constant wondering as to whether 'everything was random and chance' in a world unvisited by God, or whether there could be 'signs' and miracles whereby the 'aches of the world' are 'secretly mended'. The desolations of life can seem like 'striding round nothingness when no God spoke'. According to Isabel's poet father, 'anything can happen, it's all chance'. But in the vision of Nicholas' artist father, 'everything God made fits somewhere'. Is his death in a fire, when he burns his paintings, an act of madness, or 'the beckoning of God'? The novel does not argue towards an answer, but it evokes alternative wavelengths for our wonder and for the range of our strangeness.

This narrative refuses to be tied down to a rational logic of events. Tragedy meets transfiguration. The extraordinary visits us within the 'miracle of ordinariness'. The four letters of the title consist of soaring words that, ironically, never arrive to Isabel, but their non-arrival does not matter. Love flourishes even in silence and perhaps as part of a divine comedy. Williams dares to glorify imagination and miracle within the everyday, and leaves us alive with questions: Do I measure myself by special moments, or by limited and burdened paths, or by some intermingling of the two? Is existence inhabited by more than we usually see? Or, as Nicholas asks, 'How do you ever know?'

THE BURDENSOME ORDINARY

The everyday is our ocean. We spend most of our lives in undramatic situations. Imagination sags. Existence is on automatic pilot. But this world of small choices is where my life is tried and tested most. A few great writers like Chekhov or Joyce or Beckett have dared to depict the ravages of the ordinary and at the same time its hidden heroism. Within the small details of each day we shape who we are and undramatic heart-learning can take place. Even death will be surprisingly ordinary – perhaps.

In these lowlands another hunger becomes possible and from it another reaching out in prayer. I know my need – of salvation in the small things. It is like the 'little way' of Thérèse. Dullness can prune the ego of pride and – almost imperceptibly – can lead me towards a gentleness with others and with the limits of life. There is a deeper source of healing in the artist-Spirit, recalling me to vision even in the commonplace context of each day. Like the other areas of experience explored here, the ordinary is a place of encounter with God. There is the tendency to despise its smallness and to value only the special: that will be the tussle at the heart of our dialogue in this chapter.

But first let us pause on an embracing of the ordinary that occurs in George Eliot's novel *Middlemarch* (to mention that masterpiece again). The story, with all its complications, is focused on the crumbling of various forms of idealism. Dorothea, the central figure, has longed to find a heroic role for herself but all has collapsed. The climax comes when she spends a terrible night in tears, and eventually sleeping, on the cold floor of her room. She realises that she loves the artist Ladislaw, after seeing him in a seemingly compromising position with Rosamund. At dawn she wakes feeling 'as if her soul had been liberated from its terrible conflict'. She has left behind her own self-centred view of the world and now knows that, in spite of her own deep disappointment, she has to go ahead and 'save' even Rosamund, whom she (wrongly) believes to be Ladislaw's mistress. Then comes an eloquent paragraph that crowns this dawn awakening to hope:

> She opened her curtains, and looked out towards the bit of road that lay in view, with fields beyond, outside the entrance-gates. On the road there was a man with a bundle on his back and a woman carrying her baby; in the field she could see figures moving – perhaps the shepherd with his

dog. Far off in the bending sky was the pearly light; and she felt the largeness of the world and the manifold wakings of men to labour and endurance. She was part of that involuntary, palpitating life, and could neither look out on it from her luxurious shelter as a mere spectator, nor hide her eyes in selfish complaining.

What is so finely rendered here is the encounter with the ordinary. Dorothea's temptation had been to imagine herself as having an exceptional destiny like Saint Teresa. Looking out at the world after the collapse of her own dreams, she feels herself drawn into the world of daily burdens – symbolised in the carrying figures of the man and the woman. Yes, the world is large but each life is so limited within a necessity of 'labour and endurance'. In other words, Dorothea's conversion has left behind the exaggerated sense of a special role in history: after the long night of her desolation she emerges into this dawn of reconciliation with the ordinary adventure of humanity.

POET AND THEOLOGIAN IN DIALOGUE

Is it possible that despite our discoveries and advances, despite our culture, religion and science, we have remained on the surface of life?

(Rainer Maria Rilke)

The primordial words which the poet speaks are gates into the incomprehensible, into the unfathomable depths of reality.

(Karl Rahner)

Rainer Maria Rilke is one of the most eloquent poets of the past century in any language. His hope was to transform the transitory into moments of exaltation and to transcend the visible into

intense inwardness. The theologian Romano Guardini won-
dered whether his magnificent energy of language had any goal
outside the self. Does 'song-existence' soar into realms of feeling
beyond human relationships? Can one really have an 'objectless'
love? Is ordinary existence so empty for the spirit? Must fullness
always call us beyond our everyday lives?

Rilke could reply that he wanted to explore both the benedic-
tions and the burdens of life. This was clear in his early *Letters to
a Young Poet*, written between 1903 and 1908, where he took on
the role of spiritual mentor for a student only eight years junior
to himself. He advised Franz-Xaver Kappus, whom he never
met, to live with his questions, indeed to 'live the questions', not
expecting answers for the intellect but moments of harmony for
the heart. Even times of guilt or sadness can lead to new wisdom, provided they are not 'drowned out with noise'. What
about love, asked Kappus? Rilke replied: it is a powerful experience but immensely difficult, something the young have to
learn. 'Let deep solitude work patiently in you and never be
absent from your life. It will act like a nameless influence,
gently shaping the self you are becoming.' And Christ? Rilke
simply said: do not put obstacles in the way of his coming.

Even if he left behind the pious Catholicism of his mother (to
whom he wrote a set of Christmas meditations over many
years), he never became atheist. He wrote early poems on Christ
as his companion, but later came to find the historical figure of
Jesus too circumscribed. Often he was hostile to institutional
Christianity as cramping the imagination. In his diary of 1898 he
wrote a poem entitled 'The Church-Generation':

> Out of his spacious, sacred splendour
> They pried God and forced
> Him into their time;
> And they surrounded and hymned him
> So that he all but disappeared
> Into their darkness.

Instead of this humanly reduced religion Rilke advocated an

'indescribable discretion' before the silence of God. He suggested that the 'first premonition of eternity' is 'having time for
love'. What are we doing here? 'Love of life and love of God
must ultimately coincide.' He wanted to forge a 'passionate
music', a song of the 'sayable, here'. His poems celebrate not
only intensity but gratitude before the wordless mystery.

Karl Rahner, the greatest German theologian of recent gener-
ations, often echoes these intuitions of Rilke. Again and again he
speaks of God as 'silent mystery', at once distant and intimate.
He saw the Church as suffering from a crisis of human depth
and he looked to the poetic word to evoke 'the human preambles' of faith. In a metaphor that would have pleased Rilke,
Rahner sees each of us as precious islands carried by the
immense 'sea of infinite mystery'. Thus everyone experiences
God in one's deepest self – even if one misinterprets that
encounter or runs from it through an unreflective life.

Rahner would differ from Rilke, however, over the worth of
routine existence. Experiences of God happen not only in contemplative adoration or in moments of special self-transcendence, but mainly in humdrum and hidden fidelities. Whenever
we live with trust or courage, we encounter the mystery of God
'in the concrete experience of our everyday life'. 'One cannot
live in pure inwardness. One cannot make oneself a pure
spirit . . . One must have concrete actions as well.' Great poetry,
said Rahner, 'exists only where one faces radically what one is'.
In his theology, poetry can reach the heart, unite the scattered
self, and prepare for recognition of revelation. Thus he shares
Rilke's desire to liberate imagination for other levels of listening.

As in other chapters, this imaginary dialogue makes no claim
to remain within the known viewpoints of Rilke and Rahner.

Beyond prisons of prose

RMR: Too many people stay within a smallness unworthy
of themselves – in a prison that gives little scope for their
humanity.

KR: I worry that people fall into a cynicism, born from frustration, because they do not find wavelengths for who they really are.

RMR: Because banality blocks their imagination.

KR: I have more respect for the ordinary than you. I see the extraordinary – which I call grace – at work in the most ordinary of situations.

RMR: One of my elegies spoke of transcending the ordinary:

> Are we perhaps put here just to say
> house, bridge, well, gate, jug, fruit tree, window –
> or more ambitiously, column, tower, or really to speak, if
>   you understand me,
> to talk in a way that these things could never imagine?

And I go on to imagine a language of love that transfigures the prose of ordinary life.

KR: Of course love has its moments of exalted awareness. These are blessings when they come. But they cannot be the measure of the quality of our hearts. Can I not love within the world of jugs and windows?

RMR: The goal is to return to the ordinary transformed. I learn that in moments of specialness – beyond the prose of the everyday.

KR: You overvalue an escapist intensity, forgetful of ordinary human situations.

RMR: And if we are capable of such intensity, what is wrong with that?

KR: It implies that unless we are beyond the prose, life is worthless. Take an example. I suffer from arthritis. I am acutely aware of it every morning as I go downstairs. I know it will not improve. Indeed I know the world around me is arthritic in countless other ways. But within these limits we have to learn to live and love.

Embracing everyday deserts

RMR: Ideals are illusions, I agree. But my hope is to reveal the extraordinary.
KR: Without embracing the ordinary?
RMR: We need to be able to soar into the heights.
KR: Most of my days are unmarked by soaring. My greatest burden is not some intense darkness but the dull and irritable self. That is the daily cross of the gospel, as I experience it. How do you see the bleak moments that we all have to live? Have they no value in your eyes?
RMR: I know them only too well. But my vocation calls beyond them. I want to transmute daily realities. Aren't you called to do something similar, as a priest of God?
KR: I need also to embrace the everyday desert, not flee from it. Even tedium can be a wisdom experience.
RMR: You find it a quasi-penitential source of growth.
KR: Not in a stoic sense, although there is a quiet daily martyrdom in all our lives. I trust that the Spirit prunes and shapes my spirit towards loving even in those dreary times.
RMR: My sense of the Divine is more exalted, ecstatic, dancing, beyond all this daily boredom.

Small is real

KR: My reverence for the everyday is grounded in my faith in God Incarnate. I relish those moments in the gospels when we are told that Jesus was 'tired'. It seems a humble realism. Do you despise times of emptiness in yourself?
RMR: I am most alive when I can give range to my fullness.
KR: So you shun life's smallness.
RMR: Often, it is true, I sense a fierce resentment against the pettiness of daily living. I feel that it is not what we are made for. My desire is to sing the high notes of our humanity, where we reach out beyond our usual selves. But I don't think I shun the simple or the small. I wrote a poem called 'The Contemplative' where I spoke of a flow of 'tepid days' being broken by a storm.

How small is that with which we wrestle;
what wrestles with us – how great it is!

Small victories can keep us small. But if we risk the more disturbing encounter, we will be defeated – fruitfully so. Like the night battle between Jacob and the angel in the Bible, the angel's 'hard hand' closes upon us and shapes us until we grow 'deeply defeated by the always-greater One'.

KR: I admire those images. Of course I need to be stretched beyond the small things by both struggle and joy. It can feel like dying but it results in living. Surely decisions are what make us what we are, not just in the big turning points of life, but in the daily choosing of attitudes, the constant conflict between yes and no.

RMR: Looking at the torso of Apollo, I wrote, 'You must change your life'. The invitation to transcendence is always there but usually ignored.

Paralysis or poetry?

KR: A Christian theologian sees all change, ultimately, in the light of the surprise of Christ. One of my fears is that artists easily become allergic to the concreteness of the Christian vision. They opt for a threshold stance: they stand there, respectful but paralysed, at the entrance to mystery. The yes of faith can seem too facile.

RMR: We know too much about too much. How could we opt for such a simple answer to such huge complexity? Yes, there is a deep hesitation in me to see the figure of Christ as the totality of truth.

KR: For many people the gospel appears too definite, too human, too shocking in its claim that God became one of us, in one limited culture, in one limited life.

RMR: Even if I could accept the Incarnation, the Church has robbed Christ of depth and turned him into doctrine. Average Christianity is so seldom touched with contemplative fire.

KR: Most of my work in theology has tried to restore a spiritual dimension to doctrine. Behind the 'truth' of Christianity lies religious experience, which, I admit, we have tragically neglected. More universal than Christianity itself is the hidden creativity of the Spirit through every person. Theology tries to put worthy words on what we live without knowing it.

RMR: Where can we find those 'worthy words'?

KR: We need poets to give us speech for mystery. And you do that, even when you reject the rind of religion. But Christ is a human poetry that goes beyond words, where incomprehensible love comes near in a totally new way.

RMR: The divine 'unsayable' becomes – partially – 'said'.

Upward or downward journeys

KR: A theologian, like a poet, wants to transform life. But there are two ways of doing so. One goes upward beyond the usual world. The other goes downward into the drama of the world. One seeks a timeless and ideal vision. The other embraces a limited life within time.

RMR: Surely all religion seeks what is timeless.

KR: Christianity is more than 'religious' in that sense. It is rooted in history. It starts from the descent of the Incarnation. It sees the smallness of each day as the theatre of our transformation. A Christian is wary of timeless moments as sources of salvation.

RMR: I confess to preferring that upward quest. My desire is to celebrate the radiance of life. For me poetry like prayer means suddenly being on fire. Is there something wrong with that?

KR: Only if it rules out the finite world, the river of the ordinary. Our real drama lies there. Is life not always temporal and limited?

RMR: Terribly and tragically limited. Is religion not about seeking the eternal?

KR: Within the confines of time – at least for now. Sometimes I look at the mess of my room and say to myself, 'This is it, this is the setting of your salvation!' It is true but it is not the whole story. The terribly ordinary is part of the return journey, the ascent in love towards God.

Shields of wisdom

RMR: We are both battling against amnesia of the spirit. We do it in different ways.

KR: The world is too much with us and (as someone has joked) there has never been so much world. We are in danger of trauma. Of being overwhelmed and confused. Of suffering passivity and panic. We need shields of wisdom.

RMR: And you imply that my wisdom transcends the everyday and that Christian wisdom has to descend into the smallness.

KR: How did you know!

RMR: Because I recognise the difference between us. I see it as symbolic of two paths people take.

KR: One is incarnational and the other?

RMR: More withdrawn and more lonely, because it cannot be sure of those Christian anchors.

KR: Because of that Christ-anchor I am thrown into the drama of the definite. Where you speak, so honestly, of loneliness, I move within a relationship. All is relationship.

RMR: In time and out of time, it changes everything for you. I can imagine it but I cannot share it.

KR: And yet the worlds in which we move are so painfully small, so ordinary.

RMR: We live a daily pendulum of presence and absence, until we glimpse the peaks of wonder.

REFLECTION SPACE

Here I want to put together two different voices and at greater length than in other chapters. One is the Irish poet Patrick Kavanagh, a celebrant of the wonder of the commonplace, and the other is Baron Friedrich von Hügel, the great lay Catholic thinker.

What is offered here echoes the Ignatian practice of 'examination of consciousness'. This is a way of situated prayer within ordinary life: I listen to the tone that has dominated in the hours I have just lived, seeking healing of egoism and wisdom for the tasks ahead. It is a prayer of gratitude and realism, that serves as a quality control for my responses and as a learning to see the guidance of the Spirit in the everyday. By pausing to 'test the spirits' in this way, petty moods can be recognised and reversed through a glance in the direction of Christ or through a remembering of those who carry heavier burdens. Through a quick 'radar' of my attitudes, the heart's compass can be adjusted and the decisions that make up each day can connect more generously with God's hopes. This habit of taking-time-out for a prayerful review of the flow of daily life can be strangely fruitful in overcoming minor addictions of mood or the 'driven' quality that can take over one's disposition.

In this spirit I want to quote and paraphrase some of the wisdom of von Hügel's fascinating *Letters to a Niece*, where he shares his own spiritual life with Gwendolen Greene.

'Dispositions are the means to acquiring reality', especially the reality of God, and then 'we grow in our own smaller reality', always within a 'humble, daily, fight with self'.

You can know that this prayer is genuine if 'in coming away from it, you find yourself humbler, sweeter, more patient'. 'It is the difficulties and dangers in people that make them saints.'

'It is through ordinary non-religious moments that imperceptible grace finds material to work in and on'. God 'loves the average very much – the poor little virtue, the poor little insight'.

'It costs to live this richer life – strife and adaptation – even in such a community as the family. But how false it is to presuppose that life should be cheap.'

'Everything you do and every situation is God's call: it will all become the means and instruments of loving, of transfiguration . . . But it is for God to choose these things . . . and it is for Gwen, just simply, very humbly, very gently and peacefully, to follow that leading.'

Where von Hügel is wise and down to earth, stressing the erosion of the ego with everyday currents and calls, Kavanagh is a poet of intuitions of surprise about God's 'ordinary plenty' even in barren landscapes. He returned again and again to the simple power of imagination to reread reality and to reveal the extraordinary hidden in the everyday. Ultimately to see as God sees. He looks on the waters of the canal

> Pouring redemption for me, that I do
> The will of God, wallow in the habitual, the banal.

In 'Nineteen Fifty-Four' he is comically fighting against the fragmentation of events:

> O I wish I could laugh! I wish I could cry!
> Or find some formula, some mystical patter
> That would organize a perspective from this hellish
>   scatter –
> Everywhere I look a part of me is exiled from the I.

In a poem entitled 'From Failure Up' he asks:

> Can a man grow from the dead clod of failure
> Some consoling flower
> Something humble as a dandelion or a daisy,
> Something to wear as a buttonhole in Heaven? . . .
> O God can a man find You when he lies with his face
>   downwards
> And his nose in the rubble that was his achievement?

In another poem, 'Question to Life', he finds wonder in every small event:

> So be reposed and praise, praise, praise
> The way it happened, and the way it is.

CHAPTER 7

GATHERING THE STRANDS:
A BRIDGING MEDITATION

What matters is not what happens but how one responds to what happens.

(St John of the Cross)

Whatever happens in life to open up our natures to the tendernesses of life is redemptive.

(Bernard Meland)

Our chapters so far have sounded five notes in the chord of human growing. Each note involves a crucial dimension of who we are. We seek relationships. We fall below our best hopes. We are painfully aware of the world's pain. We spend much time alone. Mostly we live ordinary lives. Stated like that, these seem banal realities. But great literature has taken these experiences and disclosed oceans of drama and complexity. Relationships expose us to passions and surprises. Failures leave us burdened with guilt. The tragedy around can provoke numbness but also heroism. Solitude can be empty or liberating. The everyday is a crucible of our attitudes. Again, a set of platitudes, if expressed in this way. But imaginative writers, like prophetic voyagers, have revealed depths within these areas of common experience.

The intuition of these pages has been that if we are not in

touch with these deep essentials, we lack human starting points for religious faith. The rhythms of our culture can keep us disconnected from ourselves and hence disconnected from God. We have looked to the power of imaginative literature to help us re-enter our hearts, because if we can get in touch humanly, we are more deeply attentive for the hearing from which faith is born.

'Prospective Immigrants Please Note', the title of a short poem by Adrienne Rich, echoes the signposts that one used to find at, for example, Ellis Island in New York. I once heard her reading this piece, prefaced by the comment that she had more interior journeys in mind. It explores a crossing of thresholds in the quality of one's life. There are challenges to confront and choices to be made. Even if you do not go through this door, you can continue 'to live worthily', 'to maintain your attitudes',

> but much will blind you
> much will evade you
> at what cost who knows?

These lines capture the quiet paralysis where life no longer expands into newness. They express a vague sadness when diving deeper stops – through lack of courageous imagination, or perhaps through lack of a 'soul friend' (as the Celtic tradition might say). And the poem implies that I may not even realise the wealth of horizons that I have missed.

In this spirit we can summarise those five zones of experience in order to see some unifying strands:

The joy of friendship: I reach out, relate and can love. If I risk the journey of intimacy that will change who I am. But sooner or later true friendship and love will call for a quality of mercy – for the forgiving of inevitable hurts.

Owning egoism: Inside ourselves we are burdened, fragile, hurt, guilty, impotent. We carry all that vulnerability. Yet a facing of failures, within a context of trust, goes beyond self-guilt to become real sorrow.

Cries of pain: I look around and see famine, fragmentation, oppression, and the tragedies that descend on people in more hidden ways. Can my shock before the world's pain overcome impotence and become courageous commitment?

The self-journey of solitude: Will I enter a darker silence, where mere understanding disappears and where another wavelength of presence takes over?

The daily classroom: This is where I embrace the limits of the everyday or else resent them. Can a slow transformation of ordinary attitudes come about under the guidance of the Spirit?

PARADOX THRESHOLDS

What we truly are must feel like some suspended wonder, or kind of expectation.

(Ralph Harper)

Relating is at the heart of what is redemptive, and what may bring about the transformation of the world.

(Mary Grey)

On reflection each of these five zones is a potential door into depth. Each of them involves a threshold to cross, a paradox to confront, and a promise of new relationship.

In each of these journeys comes a threshold that causes fear. I glimpse how fragile everything is. I run up against my spirit of refusal. There is a sense that more is possible and that more is being asked of me. Either there is a letting go and a risk-taking, or I settle down in unrecognised half-life. Growth costs and hurts.

For instance, on the road towards love, a time of light often gives way to some darkness. You set out in the sunshine of friendship and its flow. But if you stay faithful long enough, the road becomes more uphill. Storms threaten. Not to face the challenge is to court the standstill suggested by Adrienne Rich's poem. But 'if you go through' towards vulnerability, all is changed, changed utterly: a different space of belonging is born.

Another significant moment comes when you cross the threshold from control into compassion. The heart's wavelength changes. The illusion of having answers crumbles. A quiet wonder takes its place. The manager dies and vulnerability comes to life. This shy space of helplessness is a source of deep humanity.

And of humility: it is close to what the gospel means by the poor in spirit. It echoes King Lear's tenderness or Ivan Illich's forgiveness. It is the most crucial of conversions, and it happens again and again in life. Without it I remain on the surface of myself, at a distance from the real drama of the heart, incapable of depth or prayer. But if I cross this threshold, all converges towards faith, hope, love.

There is a further horizon to all this opening out. It involves not only thresholds to cross but recurring and crucial paradoxes to be faced. The heart has to learn that going further means letting go, and that letting go is life-giving. At each threshold, the temptation is to shy away. We are experts at avoiding risks. The great geniuses of literature knew about that. They are forever dramatising the crisis of life when it runs into the shock of depth – from Emma's finding of love-clarity beyond shame or Dorothea's miracle of generosity beyond the collapse of all her hopes. Are we alone at these crossroads? Do we run? Do we cross?

When thresholds are crossed and paradoxes embraced, new relationship is always the signature of authenticity. All the ups and downs of our meandering story are validated by a freedom for mutual belonging and mutual gift. This is the test and fruit of any genuine growth. This is the only credible happy ending.

CHRISTIAN HORIZONS

> Jesus unveiled the depths of spiritual power that are avail-
> able to all who share his humanity and are willing to live
> with the kind of authenticity he showed.
>
> (Donal Dorr)

Besides, there is a Christian reading of these narratives of our lives. At these paradox thresholds, the Spirit is creative, waiting to write a divine story, even before we know it to be divine. Everyone is being saved – secretly as it were – whenever there is a birthplace of 'yes' in one's life. To use biblical analogies, our human passovers are both preparations for grace and places of grace. The adventure of exodus happens in experiences such as friendship or humility or solidarity or solitude, or in the calls of the everyday.

The full Christian story takes us still further: we are offered a less hidden Presence and Word, above all a new Relationship. The trust to cross human thresholds is the work of the Spirit; so also is the crossing of the threshold into faith. As Bernard Lonergan put it, the Spirit is 'the transformation of you so that you can listen to Jesus'. Our heart-learning is the quiet theatre of the Spirit but it also steers us towards the fullness of Christ's light. Indeed the human poetry of life as lived – in its depth and struggle – prepares us for the shock of Crucified Love.

To reach the threshold of mystery, these pages have taken the indirect route of the human adventure in its heights and depths. Not just to be ready for God but to be in touch with those expe-riences where we already meet the Spirit of God. Because God is love, not passive but flowing, energising, transforming. Like a work of beauty to the power of infinity. Like ourselves at our full range of wonder and of giving, and yet beyond all our imagining.

The question is often posed: what difference does Christian faith make? If we respond lovingly, even without knowing it, to the promptings of the Spirit in our humanity, is that not enough?

That question was put to perhaps the most saintly person I have ever known. He answered with an intriguing parable.

'Suppose I asked you to carry a bag for me and leave it in a house down the road, and suppose you generously did that, that would be good. If you thought there was just rubbish in the bag but you carried it because I asked you, that would be good. But if you knew there was gold in the bag, it would make a difference! To know the worth of what you are carrying changes everything.'

Changing the metaphor, perhaps there is an 'eyes open' spirituality, where we embrace life and answer its calls, without necessarily recognising the gold. Then there is an 'eyes closed' spirituality, where we relish the presence of God in Christ – the surprise of gold. From that is born an 'eyes open again' spirituality: we are sent into life with the gold of God's light – on who we are and why we are here.

REFLECTION SPACE

On this occasion the summary of thresholds-paradoxes-conversions-relationships can take the form of a prayer-meditation. It also points forward to the specifically Christian horizon of the next chapter.

> Lead kindly light –
> Where I prefer the admiration of others, lead me into
>   vulnerability;
> Where I prefer to hide the hurt, lead me beyond guilt into
>   sorrow;
> Where I prefer to help from afar, lead me into a sharing of
>   the pain;
> Where I prefer smooth paths of faith, lead me in disturb-
>   ing and dazzling dark;
> Where I prefer peaks of enjoyment, lead me also through
>   tired normality;

Where I prefer safety without struggle, lead me to follow
  your full road.

And yet, beyond all those thresholds, you promise
A friendship that endures,
A forgiving that reaches all woundedness,
A carrying of burdens that become light,
A resting in the strangeness of love,
A treasuring of the limits of life,
And being with you in all dying and all rising.

CHAPTER 8

THRESHOLDS
IN FAITH

You could translate all this loneliness, this groping, this dreadful bloody buffoonery into Christian terms that will make life bearable for us all. And yet you don't say a word. Why Canon, arid Canon? Isn't this your job? To translate.

(Brian Friel, *Philadelphia Here I Come*)

Theology will be doing its job when 'God' connotes that wine without which life is tepid water.

(Sebastian Moore)

After exploring five major strands of the human adventure – friendship, guilt, tragedy, solitude and ordinary living – it is time to stand at a final threshold. Does the human mystery exhaust who we are, with our depth and creativity and also our shadows? Or are we spoken to from beyond ourselves? Can we imagine being part and partners in a larger drama? The human adventure, when visited in depth, led to various thresholds of conversion. They seemed to point towards God. Now it is time to ponder the Christian possibility – that life is held and healed within a Love made Human for us.

CONTRASTING TONES

Much talk about God gives the impression of a Power Up There – sometimes friendly and sometimes menacing. As Samuel Beckett expressed it, in the mouth of Lucky in *Waiting for Godot*, we imagine 'a personal God quaquaquaqua with white beard', outside time, who from the heights 'loves us dearly with some exceptions for reasons unknown' and, we are told, suffers with those who are plunged in torment. ('Quaquaquaqua' is a nonsense word to mock all the jargon of God-talk.) As Lucky's speech descends into incoherence, its gibberish conceals an agonised summary of the human condition: 'in spite of the progress' and of a long comic-chaotic list of sports, 'man . . . wastes and pines' and 'for reasons unknown' there remains at last 'the skull'. This is Beckett's evocation of basic realities: history only seems to improve; meaning is unattainable; humanity is shadowed by decay and ultimately death; and God, if One exists, remains aloof and capricious. Beckett was a great comic and tragic voice for human longing and ultimately for loneliness without light. One of his cherished comic remarks came from something overheard on a building site: 'Don't come down the ladder, I've taken it away!' With the ladder of meaning unavailable, Beckett imagined us dangling between suffering and boredom, and forever haunted by God's absence.

For an alternative image of God I draw on another Irish writer. Aidan Mathews' short story entitled 'The Figure on the Cross', which was dramatised some years ago by BBC television for transmission on Good Friday, creates one of the best evocations of prayerfulness in fiction. It tells of a fourteen-year-old boy called Freddie, who each day visits a church on his way home from school, and has conversations with a life-size statue of the Crucified. The aggressive parish priest (Father Leo) is deeply suspicious: the boy can be up to no good. His more benign assistant (Father Phil) sees him as harmless and a bit lonely. Their comically different interpretations provide an external frame for the conversations between Freddie and Christ, which unite intimacy with everydayness:

'My dad says he has no time for religion.'
'The prophets were like that too,' said the Figure on the Cross.
'Because my dad says so many people have been killed in the name of God.'
'It happened to me.'
Freddie couldn't think of anything to say to that, so he breathed as warm as he could on the chilled feet of the figure.

Later the story enlarges its horizon to Christ's sharing in all human struggle, in its cruelty and in its giving birth to new life:

'Why were you crying when I came in?'
There was a little silence . . .
'A child in a suburb of Stockholm was struck for no reason so that her ear-drum burst and bled. Seconds before you arrived.'
'That was awful,' Freddie said.
'In a stony field on the island of Inishbofin, a fieldmouse is having her baby. Her tiny face is full of concentration. She can think of nothing else. And the planets circle her silently. They know their place.'

In a few simple words Mathews has captured the span of divine love, ranging from human disasters to that sense of cosmic reverence over the birth of a tiny animal. His story ends with Freddie offering to ease Christ's pain by taking out one of the nails, only to be caught in the act by Father Leo . . . And after he has hammered back the nail, his final, ironic words to Father Phil are 'It would take a miracle to move that now'.

Apart from the delightful way in which Mathews shows the clergy out of their spiritual depth, the image of God here suggests *the* Christian antidote to the typical God-talk satirised by Beckett. It combines two dispositions essential for a Christian wavelength: it situates itself *within* the experience of faith as relationship, and it beautifully captures the 'unless you become as a child' of the Gospel. Indeed Aidan Mathews in another context has offered an eloquent statement of his creed (with some significant word play):

> I believe that we are adored by the living mystery we dare to call God. I believe that God invites us to take this dear cherishing of us at his word and to live always and everywhere in the spirit of it, giving and forgiving along the way so as to divine at long last our own human nature. I believe this word of pledge and promise from God – the word that we are loveable and loved – to be spoken and broken most bountifully in the life and death and real presence of Jesus of Nazareth, that this person is the high point of God's passion for us . . .

But Beckett's voice necessarily returns to trouble us. The silence of God remains disturbing. It often seems an absence more than a presence. Faith can seem so frail, like a hangover from another time. To repeat: only from within the flow of love does it take flesh. What to do when the mosquitoes of doubt descend? The wisdom of imagination would say: trust the silence, wait, nourish the loving, and don't deny the dark questions that will surely come.

EVANGELISING GOD

Into all this struggle comes the figure of Jesus Christ. Pascal remarked that for a religion to be true, it must have got to know human nature. If so, divine match-making becomes complete in Christ. Many of those who honestly cannot believe, like Nietzsche, still write pages of tender admiration about the Jesus of the gospels. His story speaks to the whole range of our human story, even for those who cannot see him as fullness of light and meaning.

How do we recognise these threshold moments? Not by their intensity but by their fruits, when they quietly open the flow of our freedom and our goodness. Great writers offer variations on that emergence – satirising our smallness and dramatising our struggle towards wider landscapes of the heart. When life flows generously or courageously, we know we are on the right road. In such moments we are closer to glimpsing the One who speaks a Word that changes everything for us.

Although God is beyond all our imagining, we are *capax Dei* said Aquinas – capable of God, able to encounter the One who is so different. So far this book has explored certain human experiences as gateways towards God: experiences of depth, whether in the quiet of the daily routine or in profound moments that come more rarely. Such experiences can lead us beyond cramped images and towards the surprise called revelation. But, one may ask, is 'towards' the whole picture? Revelation also happens within the human drama of our choices. Grace encounters us within the human.

The Gospel Jesus liberates us and 'God' from the sub-Christian pictures that inhabit our imagination. Jesus evangelises God, so to speak, because the only God worth believing in meets us along a different wavelength. Not of Power but of Presence. Not of Distant Majesty but of Passionate Artistry, like a sculptor carving love-shapes out of resisting stone. Not of ritual Religion but of a Reality more real than myself. Not aloof from the human chaos but the shocking figure recognised by the centurion at the Cross: truly this man was Son of God. This is the greatest of all paradox thresholds. Crossing it will entail leaving behind the always lingering immaturity of our God-images.

CONVERSION OF THE EGO

As a final literary example from Ireland, James Joyce's 'The Dead' offers unexpected light. It is the last story in his collection

Dubliners. Most of the previous stories end with a negative insight (or 'epiphany' as Joyce called them), where the central character comes up against a sense of paralysis and hopelessness. In 'The Dead' the ending is different. It tells of a Christmas party where Gabriel Conroy, a writer and nephew of the ladies who host this occasion every year, has a somewhat frustrating evening of small failures. At the end he goes to a hotel for the night with his wife Gretta, hoping to make love with her. Earlier he had noticed her listening with a special intentness as someone sang 'The Lass of Aughrim'. Now Gretta seems withdrawn and he asks her why. She bursts into tears and tells him that the song had brought back memories. To his shock she tells him that it reminds her of a boy she knew when she was young. Gabriel's tone remains 'ironic' and 'cold' as he asks her about this boy called Michael Furey, until the full truth hits him: Michael had died for love of her. Although the boy was seriously ill, he had come in the rain to stand outside her window on her last night at home, only to die a week later. Suddenly Gabriel feels 'shy', his small ego transformed into gentleness by the memory of this event.

> She was fast asleep. Gabriel, leaning on his elbow, looked for a few moments *unresentfully* on her tangled hair and half-open mouth, listening to her deep-drawn breath. So she had had that romance in her life: a man had died for her sake. It hardly pained him now to think how poor a part he, her husband, had played in her life. . . . *Generous* tears filled Gabriel's eyes. He had never felt like that himself towards any woman, but he knew that such a feeling must be love. [my italics]

Seen in this way, 'The Dead' is a conversion story, where the self-enclosed ego is liberated through glimpsing another horizon. The contrast of his life with the story of Michael allows Gabriel to dive deeper, not into self-guilt but into generous sorrow. Another quality of love has entered his world. Although it may not have been the author's conscious intention, this ending seems profoundly Christian. It shares the pattern that St Paul expressed with such simplicity: 'he loved me and gave himself for me' (Gal. 2:20).

TOWARDS THE CHRISTIAN CORE

Everyone can love Jesus, as long as he is not God. But Jesus who is God is too difficult and demanding . . . [Before] a God so passionate he has to be Jesus, a Jesus so passionate he has to be God . . . there are only two possible responses: utter faith or utter rejection.

(Rosemary Haughton)

We generally find it easier to understand what is complex: what is simple is too demanding

(Hans Urs von Balthasar)

The central vision of Pope John Paul II in *Redemptor hominis*, his first encyclical letter, was that Christ reveals to us who we truly are – people who 'cannot live without love'; he added that humanity constitutes the 'main road that the Church must travel' in order to make this real. This book also has viewed the human as *the* road towards Christianity. In that spirit I want to evoke an encounter with Christ himself and, yet again, to do this through an imagined conversation. If there were risks of artificiality in previous dialogues, on this occasion there is a danger of falling short of the poetry needed for Christ. The goal is to put Christ and 'the Self' in contact, where the Self is not myself but rather any contemporary person of searching sensibility.

As inspiration for this exchange I take George Herbert's 'Love', which Simone Weil described as the most mystical poem in any language. It is not mystical in the sense of exploring ecstatic experiences. Its power lies in its utter simplicity. It tells of an invitation to a feast, of the uncertainty of the guest, and of the gentle insistence of the host. As a miniature drama of God's initiative and of human hesitancy, it has no equals. The rhythm of the verse captures the unease of the soul – through hesitant or broken phrases and lines – in contrast with the steady advance of love-as-host, who gently undermines the reluctance of the newcomer. At first 'quick-eyed' or sensitive in noticing the guest's embarrassment, Love comes closer, and later smilingly holds hands. Finally, the typical relationship of saviour and saved is reversed as Love insists on serving the guest, now seated as a symbol of surrender to the gift of love.

> Love bade me welcome; yet my soul drew back,
> Guilty of dust and sin.
> But quick-eyed Love, observing me grow slack
> From my first entrance in,
> Drew nearer to me, sweetly questioning,
> If I lacked anything.
>
> 'A guest', I answered, 'worthy to be here.'
> Love said, 'You shall be he.'
> 'I, the unkind, ungrateful? Ah, my dear,
> I cannot look on thee.'
> Love took my hand, and smiling did reply,
> 'Who made the eyes but I?'
>
> 'Truth, Lord, but I have marred them; let my shame
> Go where it doth deserve.'
> 'And know you not', says Love, 'who bore the blame?'
> 'My dear, then I will serve.'
> 'You must sit down', says Love, 'and taste my meat.'
> So I did sit and eat.

Although it goes beyond the situation of Herbert's poem, the conversation here starts from hesitations over faith and then moves into exploring some gospel surprises. Jesus was a 'recogniser' of our riches. He awoke people by his parables and by his presence to their hidden hopes. Then they were ready for the different God he brought them. But there was another surprise:

this healer was on the road to Jerusalem. We wanted a saviour who was gentle and peace-giving: which Jesus was, but not only. So there are two quite different movements in the gospels, rather like two movements of a symphony. If the first part is expansive, (the play on words is tempting) the second is expensive. This is a strange road that lies beyond any 'merely human' poetry of faith.

Healed into hope

> With an adorable, never-ceasing energy, God mixed Himself up with all the history of creation.
>
> (John Henry Newman)

Self: Are you really there? Or is faith illusion? You stay so silent.

Jesus: I speak only when you are ready to hear – out of respect for your freedom.

S: You should interrupt more often.

J: I am always there, creating in quiet. I am closer to you than you are to yourself. I wait for you to come closer to me.

S: I'm not ready and you know it.

J: You are not ready but it does not matter.

S: I need a wedding garment to enter your feast. They are your own words.

J: You do not barge into the feast as if you had a right to be there. Humble hunger is the best garment. Why are you so hesitant?

S: The gulf of faith is hard to cross and my own unreliability haunts me.

J: If you cling to self-doubt, you could miss the surprise of my gift.

S: When you look at us, at me, what pains you most?

J: The unlived life. The prison of smallness. And more terrible evils that spring from the shrinking of the heart.

S: Into all this, you say that you bring forgiveness.

J: Healing your wounds of refusal. Letting you discover your full story.

S: It is so easy to lose focus.

J: Stay in touch – like a child – with life, with your self, with the pain of the world. . . along many roads you can 'come' to Me.

S: Where does meaning shine through?

J: Every day, if you have eyes to see, you can come grateful from the field of life, having glimpsed the goodness of people, the courage of the poor of spirit. You can come hurt by the disappointments of the journey.

S: When I fall into staleness, I wonder whether I will ever have eyes to see.

J: Emptiness is no obstacle if you offer me the honest key to your heart.

S: And if I do?

J: Then I embrace you into healing. I let you know, beyond all usual knowing, that you are tenderly loved. I draw you to read the world with a heart that cares for the weak. I prune you and prepare you for the buffeting of life. I lead you towards my Father's house, which is your home.

S: My unsteadiness makes that road so slow.

J: Only slowly can you learn to flow with the glory that I myself received.

S: Glory is too high a word for me. My life is dullness much of the time.

J: Most of my life was 'hidden', ordinary, not mainly 'religious'. It was there that I learned to read the limits of each day with love.

S: Why did you need your nights on the mountain?

J: To live that love needs watered roots. In silence I rested in the fullness that I had known from the beginning.

S: But we are not like that.

J: I came to show you humanity at full stretch. In me you discover who you can become.

S: You are a mirror of who we are?

J: More like a surprising glimpse of where you can go – in companionship with God. It may take a lifetime to trust that We enfold you always.

S: We?

J: I am not alone. I am in my Father. My Spirit dwells within you. The dance of our love surrounds you. If only you knew.

Adventure in companionship

> God is not a secure God up there telling everybody what to do, but a God in anguish, yearning for love; a God who is not understood, a God on whom people have put labels.
>
> (Jean Vanier)

S: When I stand outside myself, examining all from a distance, you become incredible.

J: Satan's strategy in the desert was to tempt me to view life outside any relationship, without depending on God. He wants us unrooted in any belonging. But you have also known the consolation of being truly inside your heart.

S: It is like a return to harmony in music.

J: When you are in touch again with love, you know, infallibly, that I am shaping your life.

S: From inside all is marked by gratitude, wonder, gentleness.

J: You can learn wisdom from that pendulum of your spirit.

S: It is a truth I could never prove to other people.

J: The poor in spirit were ready for my companionship. The comfortable were protected against me. The religious experts were the most shielded of all, reducing all to a system.

S: A system seems safer than a life-called-out.

J: All is exodus into love. And that exodus is life-giving and life-costing.

S: When we fall into forgetfulness, what can awaken us again?

J: Saints are my subversive prophets. They reveal the whole drama of falling-in-love. They disturb the routines of religion.

S: Today we seem unsure of anything that does not make sense within our framework.

J: A truth of your own shaping will never satisfy your heart. The only meaning worth living for comes from beyond you.

S: You invite us on to risky roads.

J: Learning to love is always risky; without that risk you do not really live.

S: Is that what we avoid – the cost of love?

J: Perhaps you are simply afraid – afraid that you could never surrender your life.

S: Is that what faith is? A surrender to your dark call?

J: My 'yes' to you empowers you for everything that comes. Faith is your 'yes' recognising my larger 'yes' to you.

S: I say that full 'yes' from time to time, but it seems like a lighthouse beam that comes and goes. Then I lose courage with what seems impossible.

J: It is impossible on your own. My steady 'yes' is the light beam that matters.

S: In that school of trust I am a slow learner.

J Within your unsteadiness my imagination finds scope. I lead you, and everyone, from emptiness to fullness, with wine at Cana at the outset and with fish at dawn on the lake at the end. That is the sign of my walking with you.

Shadows and prunings

> Jesus is the only one who achieves the divine goal for all of humanity, the only person who has nothing to do with violence.
>
> (René Girard)

S: What do you want for us?

J: I want what you most want, except that you cannot always reach your real desires.

S: What blocks us?

J: Habits of low hope. A scattered existence. Secondary things that take over the heart. Sometimes a spirit of refusal born from hurt.

S: You claim to save us from all that.

J: I heal you with love and into love. Ultimately I died for you.

S: Did you have to die?

J: I lived my love in a world so closed that they hated me.

S: You were a disturber of the peace.

J: Of false peace, as the world wants. I heal you, but I also shake you and send you.

S: I am not ready for too much disturbance.

J: I never ask for what is not yet ripe. I asked nothing difficult of my disciples until they knew who I was. Then and only then did I tell them the road I had to go and the cost of coming with me. 'Whoever loses life will find it.'

S: I fear your pruning knife.

J: 'Unless the grain falls into the ground and dies, it remains alone.' Terribly alone – as when the shell stays tight closed. I crossed that threshold to open you to another kind of love.

S: That threshold meant death for you.

J: A death that gave life.

S: Can you expect us to choose that shadowed path?

J: Not as lonely sacrifice but as companionship with me. As with the bread, I take you and bless you. When I seem to break you, it is to give you in love for others. On your own the breaking seems terrible. With me the burden is light and the pruned vine bears fruit.

S: To a road of self-losing you invite us as to a feast.

J: What seems to you like surrender leads with me to self-discovery. I serve you and nourish you in every way. You need only sit and eat. All is gift.

River for a wounded world

The world of today is the Burning Bush of God's presence . . . And I am in the situation where love wants me to be.

(Egide van Broeckhaven)

S: Even humanly, we are changed most when we fall in love.

J: I take that human road and lead it further than you can imagine.

S: Beyond our reach?

J: Beyond your images of life and of God, shadowed by fear and hostility. There is another love possible. There is another God who is real.

S: Another God?

J: The flow of life that I received from the Father, I showered on you, so that you could flow with another love for one another.

S: It is hard enough to be kind. Your way is too high for me.

J: Letting go and finding is the surprise at the core of all love – from ordinary kindness to laying down one's life.

S: But it goes against the grain for us.

J: Only when you are addicted to caution. God is the opposite of caution. The river of God is love in full flow.

S: If you are that river, why did they reject you?

J: Divine flow in human form was too much for them. I was outside the game of their hatred. My freedom frightened them.

S: So they had to destroy you.

J: In a broken world love leads to the shadow of the cross. This is the dividing line in every human heart. You also have to choose where to stand.

S: You call us across impossible thresholds, into impossible dying.

J: My servant-way is senseless if you live with shrunken hopes. I entered the dark to amaze you with the flash of resurrection.

S: Where hope is released into hugeness of peace.

J: A peace that does not stay still. I send you to share it within the chaos of a wounded world.

S: Your risen love means revolution for us.

J: It is God's revolution at the heart of history. It is another logic for living. It means not death but the end of death.

S: Death still dominates us.

J: Not any more. In my rising, newness of love has already won. Death has lost its total sting.

S: And this, you say, is the power of God.

J: Which is nothing but the power of love, foolishness to the blind but wisdom to those who live it. Because I live you also can live this way.

S: Through knowing who you are, I glimpse who I am. In this gift-space all is surrounded with light.

J: You are, in your humanity, the echo of my passionate self-giving. Do this in memory of me and your aliveness will last – for ever.

REFLECTION SPACE

With gratitude to Sebastian Moore (whom I have had the joy of knowing personally), once more I borrow from his spiritual wisdom on this theme of encounter with Christ.

> We resist the impulse of the spirit to become who we truly are, the desired of God, the Christ . . . Jesus liberates us from this self-imposed captivity.

> To believe in Jesus . . . is to have one's own flood-gates opened.

A parallel sense of liberation is captured, in a different way, by the Australian poet James McAuley in his poem 'Confession', which ends:

> Bored in my self-prison
> I doubt uneasily;
> But the times when I get out,
> I know you have risen.

Again Baron von Hügel is provocative:

> Christianity is a heroism. People seem to think it is a dear darling, not-to-be-grumpy, not-to-be-impatient, not-to-be-violent life; a sort of wishy-washy sentimental affair. Stuff

and nonsense! Christianity is not that . . . Christ was no rigorist, yet he tells us to die to ourselves, to take up the Cross, to follow him. Is that all comfy?

In previous sections we have explored aspects of the human adventure that seem common to all people. Now it is possible to see how the Christ of the gospels takes and transforms these fundamental experiences.

As a revelation of new intimacy with God: 'I call you friends, because I have made known to you everything I have learnt from my Father' (John 15:15).

As a summary of healing of hurts: 'Come to me, all you who labour and are overburdened, and I will give you rest' (Matthew 11:28).

Finding Christ in all who suffer: 'In so far as you did this to the least of these, you did it to me' (Matthew 25:40).

As a glimpse into the inner silence of Christ: 'He went off to a lonely place and prayed there' (Mark 1:35).

As a summary of daily conversion: 'A follower of mine must day after day take up one's cross' (Luke 9:23).

CHAPTER 9

SPECULATIVE
HORIZONS:
SOME THEOLOGICAL
POSTSCRIPTS

If we make light of what is deepest within us . . . to *seem*
becomes to *be*.

(John Henry Newman)

The mind cannot do without analogies in its attempts to
represent God – so the door is wide open to risks.

(Henri de Lubac)

*This final chapter offers a more reflective exploration of
themes touched on in previous chapters.*

If there is widespread agreement that Europe is facing a crisis of
faith today, there remains considerable divergence over the
nature of that crisis. Among theologians and church leaders at
least six different interpretations are found, which can be syn-
thesized as follows (indeed all these tendencies were voiced at
the Synod of European Bishops in October 1999):

1. Some stress a crisis of truth: the eclipse of God is due to
   'immanentist' thinking that lacks any sense of objectivity.
   The trouble is basically intellectual.

2. Others see it as a crisis of freedom: people overvalue free-dom from obstacles to their 'happiness', but they lack goals and guidance ('freedom for'). The problems are mainly moral and cultural.
3. Others again diagnose a crisis of the person: a lonely individualism wounds people's depths and cuts them off from self-transcendence. The difficulties are more anthropological and spiritual.
4. Accompanying this is a crisis of community: people suffer from 'loss of memory', from lack of roots and of a sense of belonging. This stems from how we live together in society.
5. Another interpretation discerns a crisis within the Church itself: new listening is needed, together with honest self-critique about how the gospel is communicated. There is a lack of pastoral creativity.
6. Some commentators hope that a new language of faith may be born out of crisis. As Cardinal Danneels put it, new songs can be composed in times of exile, gospel songs in tune with the sensibility and searching of the culture. This situation calls for a discerning 'inculturation' to meet a radically changed context for faith.

In general it is clear that we face more a crisis in the language of faith rather than a crisis of faith itself (in the sense of creed or doctrinal content). And because of that, the whole thrust of these pages has been to dig down into key experiences in order to retrieve and enrich the human foundations of faith.

IMAGINATION REVISITED

Before the message there must be the vision, before the ser-mon the hymn, before the prose the poem. Before any new theologies . . . there must be a contemporary theopoetic.

(Amos Wilder)

However, there has been a central theme in these chapters that is not explicitly mentioned in those six lines of thinking. John Henry Newman claimed in one of his letters that 'it is not reason that is against us, but imagination'. And he argued more positively in *The Grammar of Assent* that 'the heart is commonly reached, not through the reason, but through the imagination'. As a young man, he had a long dispute with his younger brother Charles who had become an atheist. Through a series of letters to Charles, the future cardinal arrived at an insight that was to stay with him all his life: that an intellectual crisis always has a context of personal disposition. He told his brother: 'you never entered into the spirit of Christianity'; you are not in a 'state of mind to listen to arguments'; you are suffering from a 'fault of the heart not the intellect'. This highlighting of fundamental attitude as decisive in matters of faith evolved into the centrality that Newman gave to 'imagination'.

According to the encyclical *Fides et Ratio* there is a major crisis of truth and a serious danger of relativity. Who can doubt this? Newman would suggest, however, that this intellectual crisis has a deeper than intellectual impact. Its context is the culture, both 'high' culture and everyday culture. The pessimism of post-modern positions is echoed in lived sensibilities, or in a 'postmodernity of the street'. The gospel is blocked more by the assumptions people live by than by explicitly philosophical ideas. Of course these two levels remain interconnected in complex ways. One can wonder, for instance, to what extent relativism among intellectuals is filtered down into popular culture and mass media. The jagged rhythms of MTV (music television) seem to offer an all too accurate translation of the disorientation of neo-nihilist thought.

There is a natural tendency among theologians to pay attention to secular intellectuals and artists – looking on them as their main dialogue partners in making sense of faith. Archbishop Rembrant Weakland has voiced his worry that post-Vatican II Catholicism has not created a real culture: it has not given distinctive artistic or intellectual '*form* to our beliefs'. This is a

serious lack. And yet this important field may not be the decisive influence on faith that it once was. To a large extent the
struggle has moved from ideas to images, from theories to
lifestyles, from academies to cultures, from books to the
electronic revolution. In this new setting we need fresh images
to capture our 'orientation into the known unknown' and to
unlock the 'transforming dynamism' of our inter-subjectivity
(Bernard Lonergan).

Culture, as distinct from society, is invisible. It surrounds us
all the time and, like the air we breathe, permeates all our self-
interpretations. The culture in question here is not only the
world of art and thought. What can be called small-c culture
constitutes a less articulate, yet ever-present pressure deriving
from our ways of life. What Newman discerned as the battleground of 'imagination' is situated here and it is on this level
that perceptions of meaning and value are most powerfully
moulded. The threat, on the level of lived culture, comes from a
levelling-into-shallowness of our collective imagination. People
are not hostile to the truth at the core of the gospel, but they are
often unreachable by the usual church language. Religious
meaning has always found its most eloquent embodiment in
symbols, but today, as Eric Voegelin has argued, our symbols
of transcendence have become cut off from the experiences of
transcendence that engendered them.

This all-powerful world of media images causes dehumanis-
ation mainly to the quality of our receptivity: we come to pay
attention only to what glitters in splintered ways. The implied
message is that there is no shared human drama and hence no
depth common to us all. This book has sought to delve in an
opposite direction and to retrieve transcultural experiences of
our hungers.

Such a stress on disposition, sensibility and imagination is
essential for fundamental theology today, and in this light a different reading of the faith context is called for. If culture is a
shared 'structure of feeling' (Raymond Williams), which silently
shapes the images we live by, then a dominantly secular culture,

whether intellectual or popular, can marginalise those ways of
feeling-towards-God without which faith will remain unreal.
Old-style atheism, with its militant refusals, appears rare. The
typical cultural mood provokes an incapacity to believe beyond
ourselves. It influences what Newman would call antecedent
probabilities, those attitudinal preambles that make faith either
existentially credible or incredible.

RELEVANCE OF THE 'PRE-RELIGIOUS'

The culture may be damaging but critique needs to be voiced in
another direction as well. Sebastian Moore has remarked that
the 'ineffectiveness of organized religion today is due to its failure to speak to the pre-religious God awareness'. 'Pre-religious'
points to the whole area of openness or readiness for the word
of revelation. Where the surrounding culture causes disposition
to stay dull, or imagination to suffer malnutrition, it is small
wonder that the human grounds of faith remain weak. Today's
typical crisis of faith involves a culturally induced desolation on
the pre-religious level.

What does the pre-religious dimension imply? Most of all,
that we have an inner core of Spirit-guided desire before we
arrive at explicitly Christian interpretations of our experience.
Our hearts are being drawn towards love prior to finding the
face of Love in Christ. There is a risk of rushing into the world
of explicit religion without pausing on what is more fundamental in each of us – the experience of searching, of struggling to
live genuinely, of being slowly transformed by the adventure of
life. Here in silence and even in secret we are being shaped as
lovers: everyone, believer, unbeliever, Christian, Jew, Muslim,
Buddhist, Hindu . . .

The Spirit is the creative artist of our freedom as we move into
the flow of life. This is the zone of the inner word, the pre-
religious presence of God in each of us. Christ comes as the

embodied word, who calls us further into explicit knowing and loving like him. The two come together in a marvellous way in what Jesus said to the Samaritan woman: 'if only you knew the gift of God, and who it is that is speaking to you . . .' The gift is the universal and creative Spirit. The 'who is speaking' is the newness of Christ, the surprise of God-with-us, even-unto-death. The pre-religious dimension is like a silent poetry within people, which can often come into the open through certain moments of human experience, including those thresholds of conversion explored earlier.

When the pre-religious aspect of faith is undervalued, 'faith' is often identified with religious belief and religious belonging. Faith is something deeper and initially less definite than belief or belonging. It involves an attitude, a disposition, a range of imagination, a zone of meaning received, prior to all formulations and expression in language. Especially in today's culture, the pre-religious adventure of faith needs highlighting.

Because it has been neglected.

Because without attention to this more spiritual area of our searching and finding, the forms of religious faith lack roots and credibility within today's culture.

Because this layer of wonder is universal in people and often they have no way to recognise it.

Because one of the surprises of our post-modern moment of culture is a spiritual exploration in this pre-religious area of faith-hungering.

Because it seems a waste to train people in the externals of religion without initiating them into the wavelength of mystery at the core of religious experience.

Because the Spirit is at work in all people on this wordless level of an orientation to love and to reverence – prior to any encounter with the crowning outer Word of Christ.

The majority of people around who have abandoned regular contact with Church have not done so because of some intellectual argument against faith. They have drifted away because their imagination was left untouched and their hopes unawoken by their experience of Church. They leave less in anger than in disappointment with hollow words that claim to speak of the holy. The crisis is on the level of the 'mediation' between a tradition of faith and a new cultural sensibility. The language of the churches seems stuck in an older mode and unable to speak imaginatively to the desires of now. People need to feel themselves part of a larger Story. Like the parables of Jesus, what is needed are traps for depth, moments of human poetry that give voice to the language of desire. And this would be a response on the level of pre-religious spiritual imagination.

DANGERS OF RELIGION

Religion is dangerous to faith when it neglects its pre-religious human basis. It is in danger of losing contact with the passion and the poetry at the core of its Christian love-story. By religion, I mean the necessary structures, the organised side of our human response to God's revelation. Down through the ages religion has evolved various languages. There has been an adventure of creativity at times but at other times a tendency to fossilisation. Religion is in danger of thinking that its historically produced ways of acting and thinking are somehow God-given and permanent. This is to fall into what St Paul would call 'law' – in the sense of human traditions that can block the freshness of God's gift and its power to transform us. If that happens, religion becomes humanly hollow in its communications and spiritually stagnant in its self-security.

Its inherited languages can become a shield against God. To say this is not at all original. It is the message of the prophets at all times. They saw religion frozen into a set of pious exercises that did not transform hearts or respond to the cry of the oppressed. They were people of fiery depth who wanted passionately to release again the imaginative power of God's word.

Many people today seem starved of credible and transforming images rather than of true doctrines. Hence this book has tried to revisit that pre-religious level of imagination without which the human heart may not be ripe for faith. It has situated this drama in the ordinary but extraordinary events of life – the exodus of relationships, the failures within, the pain around, and the solitude and silence that accompanies the search. 'The image is necessary for the insight', wrote Bernard Lonergan, adding that we lack incarnate forms of truth, 'a suitable flow of sensitive and imaginative presentations'. Without meaning-as-felt, the religious enterprise can remain 'out there' and 'up there', incapable of being literally religious, of re-linking people to the Gift and Story of Love.

A DEEPER READING OF CULTURAL CRISIS

Violence can only be concealed by the lie and the lie can be maintained only by violence.

(Alexander Solzhenitsyn)

If culture is where we assimilate images of who we are, how is it that so many of those images are out of tune with the gospel? A powerful answer comes from René Girard, one of the greatest lay Catholic thinkers of today (and whose thought influences these next paragraphs). He diagnoses our crisis of pre-religious imagination in a new and provocative light. He sees all cultures as born from violence and views our desires as infected with a tendency to scapegoat others for our own evils. Culture is a vast schoolroom where we learn to desire what others desire, and in a spirit of opposition to them. Culture is where we come to imitate rivalry and distorted attitudes. What we call civilisation is never far from barbarism. Therefore all genuine religion will entail an unlearning of the hostility that rules history. In the person of Christ, in a unique way, we learn another imagination and another imitation: we are converted from copying the violent urges of our envy and towards 'positive mimesis' of the 'innocent victim', whose secret lay in fidelity to his servant-way of love.

None of the major philosophies of the West had room for this utterly different love. This core Christian image dismantles our cultural assumptions and rescues us from addiction to false images of who we are. The choice is stark – between grabbing the world in a spirit of suspicion, or being transformed through mutual giftedness. The ultimate healing of our heart's assumptions comes through the Love laid bare through the Cross of Christ. And yet before reaching that peak of revelation, there are other ways of glimpsing an alternative logic of life. Whenever we enter zones of wonder and vulnerability, we are able to see through the myth of the self-made and self-making 'man'. Or the myth that truth is merely objective – in a narrow sense. Or that freedom is merely subjective – in an equally narrow sense. The false self, fed by distorted images, exists in a shielded solitude of non-community. In ways Hobbes was right: this life is 'solitary, poor, nasty, brutish, and short'; it is 'a war of everyone against everyone' with some passing satisfaction for those who manage to come out on top.

Into all this long impoverishment of self-images – called the history of culture – comes the surprise of God's love in Christ. And through Him we gradually learn to unlearn the logic that robs our lives of their intended flow. That unlearning is called 'salvation'. The old addiction to enmity gives way to another wisdom. Ultimately we fall in love, having glimpsed that we are loved, and that indeed this flow of gift was always struggling into the open, even when we seemed to live a different set of reactions: self-shields, sulks, blaming and victimising.

Human culture, in short, is wounded by a false way of imagining ourselves. We think that death is the defining limit of life – and biologically that is correct. We allow mortality to reduce us to fear and distrust in relationships with people. An assumption of hostility reigns. Rivalry sets in and distorts our attitudes. We are so drastically wrong about ourselves, that Jesus finds it hard to make himself heard on the level at which he offers freedom.

Against all this twisted imagination, the gospels are works of revolutionary vision. They are not in the family of philosophy or of theology. They do not analyse or argue. They tell stories that reverse our way of seeing everything. Most of all they tell of a man who walks through these pages with a power that no work of literature has ever attained. His is a frightening and yet consoling presence. He disturbs all our comfortable scaffolding. We thought we knew who we were and where we were going. But this gospel Jesus invites us to a deeper joy, something our hearts can recognise, even at a distance from arriving at yes. He is in tune with our shy and half-forgotten hungers. He promises us upheaval and yet harmony. He shatters and heals our images. His presence is more like a poetic impact than a neutral truth, and faith is more a drama of the imagination than of thought or will or morality.

Human imagination has its tradition of wisdom, penultimate no doubt, but richly opening to the ultimate. The figure of Christ is both the gathering and the surpassing of the drama of human freedom, with its bewildering pendulum of splendour and destruction. And we can come to new awareness of his 'momentum of glory' (Balthasar) through the lenses of our human story in its depth. That has been the hope and pattern of this book. By re-entering our human mystery, we retrieve our antennae for God.

FROM HEART OF STONE TO
HEART OF FLESH

> In the face of suffering you are either with the victim or the
> executioner – there is no other option.
>
> (Dorothee Soelle)

> The self is so deep that it can engulf me without my
> realising there is something more . . . It is easy to see why so
> many mystics lose themselves in themselves and never
> meet God.
>
> (Yves Raguin)

An uncommitted faith is a contradiction. Newman saw that disposition was all. Lonergan insisted that 'join we must' because
'our perceiving is through our own loving'. Metz highlights the
'subversive memory' of Jesus allied to the 'memory of suffering'
in all times and places. Wittgenstein wrote that 'it is love that
believes the Resurrection'. These are conditions of possibility of
crossing the threshold from merely curious inquiry into the yes
that is faith. But that yes never ceases to wrestle with no. If the
self-showing of God is the beginning of faith, the God-changing
of us is the end. That drama is slow and daily, personal and com-
munal, hidden and historical, in time and beyond it. But Christ's
revolution finds forerunners in intuitive wisdom through the
ages. The affective conversion – from shieldedness to vulnerability and then to new tenderness – is a pattern at the heart of
great literature. Imagination glimpsed that only love can rescue
us from this culture of unlove.

Wherever people visited the human underworlds of destruction, and had the courage to imagine another light, we were
given maps for transcending our sulks. That was the journey of
Job or Dante or Shakespeare or Dostoevsky: to face the utter
dark and wait through it for a forgiving dawn. Something vital
for our humanity is at stake here: human imagination, at its best,

glimpsed how the tragic logic of evil has to be dismantled by a new logic of love. The melting moods of literature – which usually come to birth out of agony or hurt – symbolise the most generous reach of pre-religious intuition.

Both literature and revelation show that a tug-of-war goes on between two pictures of who we are – between our against-ness and our for-ness, between a cult of cut-off autonomy, and a different basis for living through learning-love. Culturally we learned to abdicate our joy, to manage our days with caution, to distrust anyone who comes too close. Automatic hostility became common sense. But in the long history of imagination contrary possibilities were always breaking through. Whenever love was discerned, in its countless and costly ways, it hinted at a sacrament of salvation. It liberated the self-doubting heart. It released the range of desire – from the bondage of grasping into the amazement of letting go.

Our long chronicle of hate, born from the habit of hostility, is one of so much inflicted pain. Imagination could create fragments of hope but it could not transform. Vergil (in Dante) could only go so far. Only grace could invite further. This is the point where the creative ascent of human authenticity meets, and needs to meet, the healing descent of God's Presence into our history. On to the tragic scene of our impotence comes One who turns out to be Love-from-God, able to embrace the logic of victimising and to overthrow it from within. On the Cross he undoes the against-ness and reveals the for-flow at the core of who we truly are. In him we glimpse what we have not dared to be and yet desire to be (Sebastian Moore). He is the Lover who dismantles the chains of culture and discloses a different Way for human living. The Servant road he chooses takes on self-hurting hate at its most naked. He becomes the Victim of all human refusing and undoes the knot that kept us prisoner from the very first sulk.

Alas, our echoing of that Christ-road remains painfully shadowed and unstable. Two moments of art can capture all this fragile fidelity. In a fine modern painting of the martyrdom of St

Stephen, the Mexican artist Juan Orozco shows a tangled mass of naked bodies in struggle. At the centre of all this movement is Stephen sinking into death, surrounded by the stone-throwers, and leaning towards the only clothed figure, who stands alone and erect at one side of the action. This is Saul (the future Paul) surveying all this violence from a height, as if approving and yet disdaining its ugliness. His tall aloofness speaks of power, pride, and the cold heart of stone. The contrast between Saul and Stephen is the daily battle of our dispositions (as well as the always tormented history of victimisers and scapegoats, as Girard would contend).

With Christ light shines into all this darkness – as the prologue of the fourth gospel proclaims. And yet the human experience of uncertainty continues. The pendulum swings between serenity and struggle. It recalls a moment at the end of Beethoven's *Missa Solemnis* when the chorus sings more and more quietly 'dona nobis pacem', 'give us peace'. It seems like a perfect, harmonious ending. But then a distant battle drum sounds. The music becomes more menacing. And the chorus explodes again, more agonised than before, more humbled in its prayer. The adventure of Christian trust is always like that.